D1642657

THE MENTAL HEALTH HANDBOOK

Tony Drew is Principal Social Worker for the Mental Health Team at Hillingdon. He has fifteen years' experience as a mental health professional. He is Editor of The Social Work Directory, published annually, and has a First Class Honours Degree in Psychology/Sociology. He is married with two children.

Madeleine King is Director of Hillingdon MIND. She has held several positions in public life, including being a member of her local District Health Authority, and is a graduate in Social Science. She has six children.

THE
MENTAL
HEALTH
HANDBOOK

TONY DREW & MADELEINE KING

PIATKUS

Contents

Acknowledgements

We would like to thank the following people and organisations who have helped us by giving information, or by reading the text and making suggestions:

Robert Brown, ASW Course Director and Mental Health Act Commissioner; Dr Dinesh Chavda, Harperbury Hospital; Jane Foulkes, Institute for Complementary Medicine; Liz Kuipers, Senior Lecturer in Clinical Psychology, Institute of Psychiatry; the information service at national MIND, particularly Sarah Teevan; Alison Pegg, Hillingdon Housing Department; Mike Roe, manager at Westminster Drug Project; SANE; Glyn Satterthwaite and Stanley Frost, Department of Employment; Dr Anthony Warren, consultant psychiatrist, Hillingdon Hospital; the many hospitals nationwide who sent us their patients' handbooks; and the large number of voluntary and other organisations who helped with the resource information in this book.

Finally we would like to thank the many users, carers and colleagues who have helped to educate and inspire us.

Authors' Note

All fees and charges quoted were, to the best of the authors' knowledge, accurate at the time of going to press in spring 1995 (although they may subsequently change, and readers are advised always to check with the organisation or agency concerned).

Introduction

Mental health problems can range from the anxiety and depression which all of us experience from time to time, to serious mental illness which can devastate the lives of individuals and their families. Many people find themselves bewildered not only by the problems which mental distress brings, but also by the confusing and complicated maze of treatments, services and professional help. This book is a common-sense, comprehensive guide to mental illness and the help available. We have written it primarily for people who may be worried about their own mental health, or that of someone close to them. We hope it will also be useful for professionals working in the field, and for the wide range of people who come into contact with mental health problems through their work or in their everyday lives.

We have tried to describe services as they really are, and to give an idea of what you have the right to expect.

The psychiatric system is largely based on an illness model of mental health. We acknowledge that many users do not see their experience as illness, but we have used medical terminology because this is what people will encounter and it is important to have an understanding of its meaning. The handbook gives detailed information about conventional medical treatment, and also covers other approaches and types of help. Everyone is an individual, and the aims of the book are to point people in the direction of the kind of help which suits them, and to give them the basic knowledge and confidence to ask questions and make choices. The days when people were expected to be passive and unquestioning in seeking medical help are gone, thank goodness. With more information and awareness the fear and stigma which still surround mental illness will, we hope, diminish.

1

Mental Health: a Quick Guide to the System

**Diagnosis and treatment • Finding help and support •
Rights and restrictions • Getting on with life**

The mental health system is made up of all the people and
organisations who work in the field of mental health, together with the laws and policies which guide their work. Mental
health care has many different facets – from medical diagnosis and treatment to practical help with money and
housing. There are also many different agencies and professional groups involved, so that the system is not particularly
easy to understand. However, although resources vary in different parts of the country, the way in which services are
organised is basically the same throughout the UK; there are
some differences in law and procedures in Scotland and
Northern Ireland, which are mentioned in the text where
appropriate. This chapter aims to give you an introduction to
some of the issues and some pointers for finding your way
around the system, as well as where to find the relevant
detailed information in this book.

DIAGNOSIS AND TREATMENT

The term **mental illness** is not straightforward. Chapter 1
explores some of the difficulties in using the 'mental illness'

label to describe different problems, not all of which call for medical diagnosis and treatment. The different forms of mental illness and their signs and symptoms are described, together with the various approaches to treatment and where to seek help. Chapter 2 gives a detailed description of psychiatric **treatments** and what they involve.

If you are worried about your own or someone else's mental health, here are some of the main points to bear in mind about diagnosis and treatment.

● many mental health problems are temporary reactions to **stress**; it is therefore important to recognise and tackle any underlying causes of stress

● **some mental illnesses are serious and may be persistent;** these conditions call for skilled assessment and treatment

● treatment involves a **partnership** with doctors or other professionals; the more information you have about effects, side-effects, and different treatment options, the more likely you are to feel confident about your treatment

● most people's starting point for discussing worries about mental health is their **GP** (general practitioner); while a medical assessment is important, it is not usually the whole answer and there are other important kinds of help and support to be considered.

● treatment in **hospital** is sometimes needed, although there is now an increasing emphasis on providing care and treatment in the community. Hospital care is described in detail in Chapter 6.

FINDING HELP AND SUPPORT

Getting access to the right kind of help and support at the time it is needed can be vital, and yet this is often a problem because of a lack of information. For example, you may be unclear about the roles of the various professionals involved in mental health care, and unsure of what help to seek from whom. Chapter 4 explains who does what and describes the roles of the mental health professionals you are likely to come across.

Wherever you live there will be some common services:

- help from **mental health professionals** (see Chapter 4)
- **counselling** and **day care** (see Chapter 5)
- **supported housing** (see Chapter 12)

There may also be other kinds of assistance, but it varies from area to area. When finding out about local resources, remember:

- there are a great many **voluntary organisations** which provide help and support; the larger national organisations are listed and described in this book (see the Index of Organisations on p. 244); there are also many small, local self-help and support groups

- the local **social services** (a department of your local authority) and **branches of MIND** are easily accessible places from which to obtain information about the whole range of local resources; **libraries** are also a good source of information

- there may be a **community mental health centre** in your area with a number of services under one roof (see p. 69)

- you can ask your local social services to arrange for an **assessment of your needs**; help should be provided based on this assessment

- **family or friends** involved in supporting someone with mental health problems may need help and support in their own right; mental health services are supposed to cater for this (see Chapter 9)

- Chapter 10 describes the **specialist help available** for people from minority ethnic communities, older people, children and young people, and people with problems related to addiction and dependency.

3

RIGHTS AND RESTRICTIONS

When you seek help from the mental health services, either for yourself or on behalf of someone else, you have various rights which are explained in Chapter 11. You are likely to find most professionals helpful, although services can be of variable quality. If you are not happy with a service you should make a complaint; advice about making complaints is also covered in Chapter 11.

Mental health problems occasionally lead to such a loss of insight or motivation that people do not seek help, even though the problems are serious. Family and friends may then be placed in the difficult position of trying to get help for a person who is reluctant to accept it. There may also be differences of opinion between the person concerned, their family and friends, and the professionals involved. In these circumstances it is important for everyone to be aware not only of the resources available, but also of their rights, and the extent to which professionals can and cannot intervene:

• **help is sometimes needed in a crisis;** Chapter 7 describes the kinds of crisis which can arise, and where you can turn to

• **for the great majority of people, care and treatment are provided only with their consent**

• the **Mental Health Act** provides the framework for compulsory admission to hospital for assessment or treatment where this is in the interests of a person's health or safety or for the protection of others; the most commonly used sections of the Act are described in Chapter 7

• carers have an important role, particularly if they are also in legal terms the **nearest relative**; see p. 133 for a definition of this term and p. 178 for a further explanation of their rights and responsibilities;

• the restrictions which can be imposed under the Mental Health Act are balanced by **individual rights and**

safeguards, for example rights of appeal to a Mental Health Review Tribunal

GETTING ON WITH LIFE

People with a mental health problem have the same basic needs as anyone else; these include having enough money to live on; decent housing; employment or occupation; satisfying relationships; and a reasonable quality of life. An approach to mental illness which relies just on medical treatment is inadequate. Mental illness can affect your ability to cope with daily life, which can lead to major problems with housing, money and employment; these problems themselves can produce stress and damage morale, which in turn can be a cause of mental ill health or can prevent recovery. So don't underestimate the significance of these areas for maintaining good mental health, and in dealing with practical problems which can arise as a result of mental ill-health. The last four chapters of this book provide information about how the system works and about help and support in the following areas:

- **housing:** there is a range of housing available for people who need extra support; Chapter 12 describes the various options and gives information about ordinary council tenancies

- **money:** mental illness can cause difficulty with managing money and can disrupt employment and earning capacity; Chapter 13 describes some of the problems that can arise and how to get help, and explains the main financial benefits available.

- **employment and training:** Chapter 14 covers the various employment and training schemes which exist for people who are trying to find work; it also discusses some of the problems which can occur in the workplace

- **education and leisure:** education and leisure can be a good

5

way of keeping in touch with other people, finding a sense of fulfilment or simply having an interest; Chapter 15 explains how you can pursue further or higher education, and gives suggestions about leisure activities

2

Mental Illness

Incidence and types of mental illness • Causes of
mental illness • Recognising mental illness • Anxiety •
Depression • Post-natal illness • Eating disorders •
Schizophrenia • Manic depression • Personality
disorders • Organic disorders

This chapter describes the main types of mental illness as
they are currently understood in psychiatry. But be warned:
it is easy to apply a label and then to look for symptoms
which seem to confirm it. It can also be easy to see 'symptoms' in normal behaviour if you look hard enough.
Objective diagnosis can only be made by a doctor with psychiatric training and experience.

INCIDENCE AND TYPES OF MENTAL ILLNESS

Mental illness affects the lives of many families. It has been
estimated that at some point in their lives one in six women
and one in ten men will spend some time in hospital for this
reason. Doctors in Britain diagnose 6 million people a year
as suffering from some form of mental disorder, and some
estimates put the figure at up to 12 million. Problems related to depression and anxiety account for most of these
numbers, although serious mental illness such as schizophrenia and manic depression is also more common than
most people think. The number of people suffering from

schizophrenia in the UK is thought to be in the region of 250,000, with a similar number suffering from manic depressive illness. Amongst older people the likelihood of suffering from dementia or severe depression increases with age: a quarter of people over eighty-five suffer from dementia. One of the problems in understanding the term 'mental illness', and making sense of the statistics quoted above, is that it is used to describe many different conditions with a whole range of causes and effects. There are also differing views about what mental illness is, and about its causes, although most mental health professionals agree that some people are genetically more prone than others to develop a serious mental illness, and that major stress can act as a trigger.

Mental health professionals often distinguish between 'serious mental illness' and other forms. People with illnesses such as schizophrenia and manic depression have periods when they experience **psychotic** symptoms, which involves losing touch with reality. Less serious mental health problems, such as those related to anxiety, stress or personality, can also lead to a breakdown in a person's normal functioning; these are sometimes referred to as **neurotic** conditions. A third type of mental health problem is often described as **organic** in origin: this means that the problems are related to a disease or injury which affects the brain, for example Alzheimer's disease which is one of the causes of senile and presenile dementia. **Personality disorder**, a more controversial classification, refers to extremes of personality which are thought to be abnormal. Finally, and beyond the scope of this book, there are disorders which are related to **learning disability** or mental handicap, which affect intellectual ability from an early age.

Classification of mental disorders in psychiatry

Neurotic Disorders (relating to stress and emotional problems)	anxiety states panic attacks phobias obsessive compulsive disorder eating disorders mild depression
Psychotic Disorders (involving delusions or hallucinations and loss of insight)	schizophrenia manic depression psychotic depression
Organic Disorders	delirium or dementia caused by physical illness brain damage drug and alcohol-related disroders
Personality Disorders	

CAUSES OF SERIOUS MENTAL ILLNESS

There is no complete agreement about the causes of serious mental illnesses. There is, however, a growing body of research which suggests that brain abnormalities are involved, and that mental illness sometimes runs in families. There is no evidence that stress by itself causes serious mental illness, although it seems to play a part in causing relapses and may be part of the total picture. Some people appear to have a particular vulnerability to mental illness because of some abnormality in their brain which they have inherited or which has been caused in some other way, for example brain damage caused by trauma during or before childbirth, or by some dietary deficiency or toxic effect. One widely accepted theory is that people who are physically vulnerable in this way are predisposed to develop a mental illness and that this may be triggered by environmental stresses (see diagram).

9

The causes of mental illness

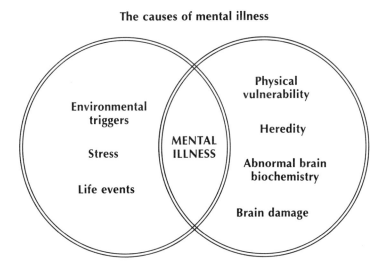

Research into the causes of mental illness has made some progress in recent years, but precisely how and why mental illness occurs remains an unanswered question.

RECOGNISING MENTAL ILLNESS

Problems of normal life

The term 'mental illness' can be used to cover a wide range of problems, and as a label it can be unhelpful and misleading. It is normal to experience stress and to react to it in various ways, for instance by feeling mildly depressed or anxious. It is normal to have personality quirks and to find it difficult at times to get on with other people. These types of problem are not likely to be the result of mental illness, and are merely part of being human. Although it may be tempting to see difficult personal problems as something which can be treated by a doctor, it is better to take personal responsibility for dealing with such difficulties than to 'medicalise' them and seek expert help.

Culture and mental illness

Most mental illnesses have been shown to occur in all cultures throughout the world, although there are cultural differences in the way in which they may present. Diagnosis is usually made on the basis of observing behaviour and beliefs which are held to conform to the signs and symptoms of mental illness. There are, however, cultural differences in people's beliefs and behaviour, in their family values, and the ways in which they behave when ill. For this reason it is essential that a person's behaviour and beliefs are seen and understood in relation to what is normal within their culture. It can be easy to misinterpret, and if a doctor is not familiar with the culture of his or her patient there is a risk of misdiagnosis. The doctor may, for example, be looking for evidence of mood disturbance or hearing voices. If the patient is a member of a religious group in which it is normal to experience altered states of consciousness or to speak in tongues, this will make a reliable diagnosis more difficult.

The experience of different ethnic groups in the UK reveals some worrying trends. Black African/Caribbean young men, for example, are far more likely to be admitted to psychiatric hospital and to receive a diagnosis of schizophrenia. There is concern that part of the reason for this is misdiagnosis, as many doctors do not have sufficient understanding of the cultural factors involved. A different concern is that members of the Asian communities use mental health services less than they need, because of language and cultural barriers, and that not enough is being done to make the services sensitive to the needs of all cultures. The Mental Health Act Commission, amongst others, has pointed to these shortcomings and professionals are gradually becoming better trained and more aware of cultural issues.

Chapter 10 includes details of some specialist services which are particularly relevant to people from ethnic minorities.

Stress

Problems with relationships, worries at work, fatigue, and financial problems can cause high levels of stress; major life events such as bereavement, divorce or the loss of a job are even more damaging. People react to stress in different ways and sometimes more serious symptoms, including some of those described below, may be experienced. This can be frightening if it happens to you, and worrying for your family and friends, but does not necessarily mean that you have a mental illness; you may need help, however, in dealing with the causes and effects of stress.

Mental illness

When faced with worrying symptoms, people react in different ways. Your instinct may be to cover up the problem or it may be to seek the reassurance of a definite diagnosis from a doctor, so that you know what the cause is and what can be done to help. Mental illness often has a gradual onset, and it can take a long time before the nature of the problem becomes clear. Because there may be other explanations for changed behaviour or distressing symptoms, doctors are usually cautious about making an early diagnosis of mental illness. This 'wait and see' approach may be very frustrating for the person concerned and their family and friends, who often experience a particularly difficult and stressful time when help and advice from mental health professionals and support groups may be most needed.

When to seek help

If the problems are serious enough to be affecting daily life, if they are persistent, or if they are causing major worry, a proper medical and social assessment should be made. For most people the starting point will be a visit to the GP, who may make a referral to a psychiatrist or other mental health professional if appropriate, and should do so if asked. If your GP is unsympathetic, go to one of the specialist voluntary organisations or the local social services for advice. (See Chapters 4 and 5 for more details about mental health professionals and the advice and support available.)

ANXIETY

Modern life can be very stressful. Anxiety is experienced by everyone at some level, and a certain amount is probably necessary and unavoidable. It can, however, become so extreme that it affects your ability to lead a normal life. Anxiety may occur in particular situations, or it may be present for most of the time. It can be experienced in various ways:

- general anxiety, where feelings of anxiety are present for most of the time

- **panic attacks,** where a rapid build-up of anxiety may lead to feelings of faintness or a pounding heart, and a fear of going out of control

- **phobias** (exaggerated fears) related to particular situations. Some of the more common ones include fear of being in a confined space (claustrophobia); fear of being away from the security of home, or in open or crowded places (agoraphobia); fear of certain animals and insects; and fear of flying

- **obsessions** may occur; these are repetitive thoughts which keep on intruding without good reason, and which the person recognises as being unreasonable

- a person may feel he or she has to act on obsessional thoughts, known as **compulsive behaviour.** Examples include continual handwashing, doing things in a particular order, and continual checking. Psychiatrists refer to this as 'obsessive compulsive disorder'.

Treatment

Anxiety can be very disabling. A GP should be able to advise on the best form of treatment and may refer you to a psychologist, psychiatrist or community psychiatric nurse. See Chapter 4 for details of what these professionals do.

- **counselling** may be helpful in looking at the causes of anxiety and how to tackle it. See Chapter 5 for general information, and ask your local branch of MIND or local social services about local resources

- **psychotherapy**, a more intensive form of talking treatment, may be helpful if the problems are severe. The treatment for phobias and obsessions usually involves specialist psychological help, for example learning deep relaxation and how to cope better, in a very gradual way, with situations which cause anxiety

- **stress control groups** and **relaxation groups** can also prove very helpful; these are often run by mental health professionals locally. Relaxation can also be practised individually, using special cassette tapes

- **complementary therapies** such as yoga, meditation and massage can be very valuable in reducing anxiety. See Chapter 3 for details

- **medication** may be prescribed, although this is not usually a first choice treatment as anti-anxiety drugs can have side-effects and can be addictive. See Chapter 3 for details

DEPRESSION

Most of us experience some degree of depression as a reaction to difficult or painful events in our lives, or in response to a personal problem of some kind. Depression may also sometimes occur for no apparent reason. It can lead to an overwhelming sense of sadness, hopelessness and loss of interest, which is distressing for the person concerned and their family. Women are twice as likely as men to suffer from depression. Research has shown that this is probably linked to social problems such as excessive family responsibilities and the lack of any close confiding relationship; this may say more about the social roles of men and women than about any inherent differences in psychiatric vulnerability.

Severe depression may produce the same symptoms as the depression which occurs as part of manic depression:

- Your normal **sleep patterns are likely to be disturbed,** and you may often wake very early in the morning

- you can experience **loss of appetite** and consequent **weight loss**

- it can be **impossible to make decisions** or take any action to help yourself

- you may be **physically slow and lethargic,** or occasionally **agitated and restless**

- in some cases **delusions** or **morbid preoccupations** may occur, for example of some impending disaster

- with severe depression you may **wish to be dead,** and may have **thoughts of suicide.** See Chapter 8 for a discussion of suicide risk

Treatment

If your feelings of depression are extreme, or if they do not go away, you should seek help from your GP in the first instance. He or she will be able to advise you on the best form of treatment, although many GPs tend to be better informed about medication than about the other forms of help for depression. Be aware of the other options, and be prepared to discuss them with the doctor.

- **counselling** or **psychotherapy** may be helpful, particularly if your depression seems to be related to social problems and stresses. See Chapter 3 for details of psychological therapies and Chapter 5 for information about counselling

- **self-help groups** may also be helpful; see p.72 for details of Depressives Anonymous and Depressives Associated. Contact your local branch of MIND or the local social services to find out about what is available in your area.

- **medication:** for severe depression antidepressant drugs may form an important part of treatment (see Chapter 3 for details)

- **electro-convulsive therapy,** although controversial, is sometimes used for people who are severely depressed and do not respond to medication (see p.37)

- **complementary therapies** may be helpful in combating depression (see Chapter 3)

POST-NATAL ILLNESS

After giving birth a woman's hormone levels change suddenly, and this, together with the physical and emotional exertion of childbirth, can cause new mothers to become weepy and easily upset. This condition, often called **baby blues,** can affect many women within the first ten days after childbirth. It is short-lived, and no treatment is needed beyond rest and reassurance.

Post-natal depression affects about 10 per cent of women and leads to a more overwhelming feeling of inadequacy, depressed mood, and loss of energy and interest. Mothers may sometimes experience thoughts of self-harm or of harming the baby. The condition can last for weeks or even months, and may need medical treatment using anti-depressant medication (see Chapter 2). Self-help groups and supportive counselling can also be helpful.

Post-natal psychosis, sometimes known as puerperal psychosis, is a rarer condition which affects between one and two mothers per thousand births. It is a serious illness with an abrupt onset. There are usually strong feelings of guilt and despair; delusions, hallucinations and mood disturbances are common. Medical treatment using anti-psychotic medication (see Chapter 3) is often needed urgently and is normally very successful, although the condition may recur in subsequent pregnancies.

See Chapter 5 for details of the Association for Post-Natal Illness, Meet-A-Mum Association, and other self-help organisations.

EATING DISORDERS

Anorexia

Anorexia is an eating problem, which frequently starts during adolescence. A person with anorexia tries to reduce their weight by eating very little, and sometimes by taking excessive exercise. A vicious circle can develop: the more weight that is lost the more the person's body image is distorted, and they see themselves as fat, resulting in even less food being eaten. Sometimes the weight loss and malnutrition are so severe that they endanger health or even life itself.

Anorexia may be a response to emotional trauma or disturbed family relationships; it can be a way of dealing with feelings of anger or guilt, or a way of avoiding dealing with other problems. It is sometimes seen as a person's way of asserting control over their body and their life, in a situation where they feel they otherwise have little control.

Bulimia

Bulimia is an eating problem which involves binges in which large amounts of food are eaten, often outside normal mealtimes and in secret. The person may continue eating until they are in physical discomfort, when they feel guilty and disgusted and may make themselves vomit or take laxatives to avoid gaining weight. The body weight is usually in fact normal, although the person sees themselves as overweight. These activities may be carried out in response to feelings of boredom or unhappiness.

Treatment

Anyone suffering from an eating problem should seek help at an early stage, normally through their GP in the first instance. Because eating disorders usually involve a very distorted self-image, the person concerned may not acknowledge that there is a problem, even though it may be distressingly obvious to those around them. Persuading the person of the need to get help can be a difficult task, and family members may need support and advice for themselves.

● treatment is likely to be based around talking treatments such as **psychotherapy** (see Chapter 3), or **counselling,** a less intensive form of help (see Chapter 5)

● if and when an eating disorder becomes life-threatening, treatment in **hospital** may be needed, with special support and supervision to re-establish a reasonable diet

● **medication** may be prescribed to help with any associated problems of depression or anxiety (see Chapter 3)

● **self-help groups:** see Chapter 5 for details of the Eating Disorders Association, and other self-help and support groups

SCHIZOPHRENIA

About one in 200 people are diagnosed as having schizophrenia at some point in their lives, usually when they are young adults – although the onset can be later. The main symptoms which doctors look for are:

● **disordered thinking,** where normal logical thought

processes are distorted; the person may be unable to focus their thinking or to concentrate on what others are saying; words can be jumbled and it may be difficult or impossible to have a normal conversation

- **hallucinations,** e.g. hearing voices when there is no one else speaking; this may be very disturbing and unpleasant, particularly if the voices are critical or will not go away; less commonly, visual hallucinations may occur, or disturbances of the senses of taste, smell or touch

- **delusions** (false beliefs which are firmly held) may include a sense of being persecuted, that you are being 'bugged' or your food poisoned, or a feeling of puzzlement that 'something is going on'

- **distortion of the person's understanding of their relationship to the outside world,** e.g. thinking that your thoughts are known to others or that you are under the control of outside forces

- **disturbance of feeling,** e.g. being emotionally blunted, or showing emotion which does not fit the situation, e.g. laughing for no apparent reason

- apart from these 'active' symptoms, there may also be a general **loss of motivation and energy, withdrawal from social relationships,** and a **deterioration in self-care.** This may happen gradually over a long period, with the person becoming more and more isolated and less able to care for themselves properly, and these problems may persist when the other symptoms have resolved

The symptoms of schizophrenia can be very distressing and can lead, as shown above, to changes in behaviour which may appear bizarre to others. Not all people with schizophrenia experience all these symptoms – in fact there is a wide range of symptoms and effects. It may be that schizophrenia is not so much a single illness but a cluster of related disorders. There is some evidence that there are two main types, one type with a predominance of the 'active' symptoms above, and the other type with a slower onset and a gradual deterioration in social functioning. The first type generally responds well to drug treatment, although some people experience periodic relapses. The second type is more difficult to treat and a lasting disability may remain.

The course of schizophrenia cannot be predicted with any certainty. Some people make a good recovery, others may be able to manage their lives reasonably well with continuing treatment, while for others the quality of life may be seriously impaired.

Factors affecting the outcome of schizophrenia

Good outcome likely	Poor outcome
Sudden onset, linked to stress	Slow, gradual onset
No previous psychiatric history	Previous psychiatric history
Age 40+ at onset	Younger at onset
Short episode of illness	Longer episodes of illness

One of the main difficulties is that the person with schizophrenia may lack insight, and their distorted perceptions may be experienced by them as reality rather than as evidence of illness. They may be very frightened and distressed by their experiences and this, together with a mistrust of what doctors and other professionals may do, can result in the person becoming guarded and suspicious and covering up the symptoms. It is not uncommon for people suffering from schizophrenia to reject help and treatment. They may also become depressed, either because of the illness itself or as a reaction to its effects on their quality of life; finally, there is an increased risk of suicide (see Chapter 8).

Treatment

Schizophrenia needs skilled assessment and treatment. The latter should aim both to reduce symptoms and to alleviate the illness's effects on the person's quality of life (for example it may have had damaging effects on their relationships, employment, housing and income).

• **medication:** treatment is likely to involve medication using antipsychotic drugs which can be effective in controlling symptoms. These drugs may either be taken as tablets, or as 'depot' injections (slow-releases see p. 31) every one to four weeks. Medication may be needed on a long-term basis, under the supervision of a GP or community psychiatric nurse and with occasional outpatient appointments with a psychiatrist. See p. 31 for details of medication used in the treatment of schizophrenia

• **community support** through day care, befriending and counselling may be needed, and is likely to be very important for those people with more severe and disabling symptoms. The National Schizophrenia Fellowship (see pp. 140–2) is a leading voluntary organisation for people with schizophrenia and their families. An alternative, user-led approach is offered by the Hearing Voices Network (see p. 87). See Chapter 3 for details of the care and support available

• **support from mental health professionals** such as mental health social workers and community psychiatric nurses may be useful in dealing with the effects of schizophrenia on social relationships, employment and life in general. See Chapter 4, and pp. 68–70, for details of the various mental health professionals and the support they offer

• **psychological therapy** can help people to find ways of coping with any continuing symptoms. A 'cognitive' approach is perhaps likely to be the most helpful. See pp. 38–40 for a description of the range of psychological therapies

MANIC DEPRESSION

Another serious form of mental illness, manic depression is sometimes referred to by psychiatrists as **bi-polar affective disorder.** The main symptom is a profound disturbance of mood, which can be either 'high' (mania) or 'low' (depression). People who suffer from manic depression can experience swings of mood which are much more extreme than the normal mood swings which affect many people. Some people are described by psychiatrists as having a **unipolar affective disorder**, which means that they experience episodes of being either high or low and do not alternate between the two.

Mania

When someone is manic they may be very elated and over-active, with rapid speech and expansive ideas. They may also be extravagant, for example spending large amounts of money and getting into debt. During these periods they may sleep less than usual, and easily become irritable and angry. They may lose their normal inhibitions and have no aware-ness of their changed attitudes and behaviour. The feeling of elation which sometimes accompanies a manic state is not unpleasant and some people are able to harness it into cre-ative energy. But often these positives cannot be sustained without serious effects on the well-being of the person and those around them. It can be difficult for the person to accept that what they are experiencing is a symptom of men-tal illness and should be brought to an end through treatment. Some of the symptoms of schizophrenia may also be experienced for brief periods. Occasionally symptoms of both schizophrenia and of manic-depressive illness occur fairly equally, and psychiatrists sometimes refer to this as **schizo-affective disorder**.

Depression

The depression which can occur may lead to a sense of over-whelming despair, guilt and feelings of unworthiness. The person may feel apathetic and totally unable to perform the simplest task, and even stop talking, eating or drinking. Thoughts of suicide may arise, and there is an increased risk of actually committing suicide (see Chapter 8 for a discus-sion of suicide risk).

Treatment

Like schizophrenia, manic depression is a serious mental illness for which skilled assessment and treatment are important. Manic behaviour can cause enormous stress and may lead to damaged family relationships. Depression may also be the cause of much stress and distress. As a result, both individuals and their families may need help and support in coping with the effects of the illness.

- **medication:** treatment is likely to involve mood-stabilising drugs such as lithium and carbamazepine, antidepressants, or antipsychotic drugs during an acute manic phase. Drug treatment can be very effective, although the drugs are powerful and need careful monitoring. See Chapter 3 for details of the drugs used in treating manic depression

- **electro-convulsive therapy** is sometimes used as a treatment for a severe episode of depression where drug treatment has proved ineffective (see p. 37 for further details)

- **community support** through day care, befriending and counselling may be very helpful in maintaining good mental health. The Manic Depression Fellowship is a national voluntary organisation which can provide information, and has a number of local support groups both for sufferers and for family members. See Chapter 5 for details

- **support from mental health professionals** such as mental health social workers and community psychiatric nurses can also be valuable in dealing with the social effects of the illness. See Chapter 4 and pp. 68–70 for details of the various mental health professionals and the assistance they can offer

- **psychological therapy** may have a role in helping to deal with the effects of the illness at a point when the person is relatively well, although it is not an effective treatment for the illness itself. See pp. 38–40 for details of psychological therapies.

PERSONALITY DISORDERS

Psychiatrists use the term 'personality disorder' to describe problems usually of behaviour, which seem to stem from a person's basic personality being flawed in some way. Most of us have some shortcomings in our personalities, and some degree of emotional or psychological damage during our formative years is not uncommon. But if this damage is severe, and the person's innate ability to recover limited, their behaviour and social functioning may be affected beyond what might be considered 'normal'. There is little doubt that some people who have been given this label find it very difficult to lead a normal and fulfilling life and are very much in need of help and support.

Numerous types of personality disorder have been described by psychiatrists, for example paranoid, obsessional, histrionic, impulsive, dependant, narcissistic and so on. These labels should be used with caution as no two people are the same and it is easy to oversimplify. They are essentially descriptions of set patterns of behaviour.

Psychopathic disorder

This is the best-known and most widely used category of personality disorder, and describes the most difficult and damaged people whose behaviour is likely to cause problems for others. Psychopathic disorder is defined in the Mental Health Act as a persistent disorder involving 'abnormally aggressive' or 'seriously irresponsible' behaviour, although psychiatrists use the term slightly more precisely to describe people who appear unable to feel guilt or consideration towards others. Some psychiatrists prefer the terms 'antisocial' or 'dissocial' personality disorder. People with this label are usually seen as lacking in personal warmth, manipulative and unable to form emotionally satisfying relationships. There is little evidence that people with psychopathic personality disorders can be successfully treated, and some psychiatrists feel that they cannot really be helped by psychiatry at all, other than to be detained in a secure setting if their behaviour makes this necessary.

ORGANIC DISORDERS

There are many **physical illnesses** which can affect mental health. Some of these effects are temporary, as with the confusion and agitation known as **delirium**, which can occur with a high fever or infection. Prescribed drugs used in treating a physical illness can also have toxic effects. Some illnesses lead to a process known as **dementia**, in which the brain function deteriorates. This condition can also be caused by vitamin deficiency.

Physical illnesses which can cause mental disturbance

- **acute infections** can cause delirium, in which a person suddenly becomes confused and emotional and may even experience hallucinations

- **AIDS**: the later stages of the disease can lead to dementia

- **Alzheimer's disease**: progressive loss of brain function, usually in old age, results in impaired memory and confusion

- **brain tumours** can cause various symptoms which also occur in mental illness

- **cerebral vascular accidents (strokes)**: these may impair brain function

- **Creutzfeldt-Jacob disease**: a disease of the brain which leads to dementia with impaired memory, loss of drive and in the later stages hallucinations

- **Cushing's syndrome**: overactive adrenal glands can cause depression

- **epilepsy**: a particular type called temporal lobe epilepsy

25

can produce symptoms similar to those of schizophrenia

- **Huntington's chorea:** an inherited disease which starts in middle age and can affect behaviour and produce symptoms similar to those of some mental illness

- **multiple sclerosis:** a progressive disease of the nervous system which can cause depression, elation, and in the later stages dementia

- **Parkinson's disease:** a progressive disease of the central nervous system which may cause dementia and depression

- **Pick's disease:** a hereditary degenerative disease of the brain similar to Alzheimer's disease, which can affect behaviour and emotions

- thyroid disorders: **hyperthyroidism,** in which the thyroid gland is overactive, can cause symptoms of overactivity and agitation; an underactive thyroid gland can lead to **hypothyroidism,** sometimes called **myxoedema,** with symptoms of lethargy and depression, and disturbed behaviour can occur

Brain damage

Damage to the brain from physical causes such as road traffic accidents can also cause different kinds of mental disturbance, including psychotic symptoms and personality changes, depending on the part of the brain affected. See p. 244 for details of HEADWAY, the National Head Injuries Association.

Alcohol

Prolonged misuse of alcohol can lead to permanent brain damage and a condition called **Korsakov's syndrome,** in which short-term memory is affected and the person is disoriented in time and place. If a person is addicted to alcohol he or she can suffer unpleasant withdrawal symptoms and can experience a state known as **delirium tremens,** with physical tremor and frightening hallucinations, usually visual, often accompanied by feelings of fear and distress. Many national and local organisations offer help and support to people with alcohol problems, before permanent damage has been done. Details of help for alcohol problems and support groups such as Alcoholics Anonymous and Alcohol Concern can be found in Chapter 10.

Drug misuse

Non-prescribed drugs like amphetamines, crack cocaine and LSD, and other mind-altering substances such as glue or magic mushrooms, can produce profound temporary mental disturbance which may even require medical treatment. Antipsychotic drugs can be used to help with some of the symptoms if they are serious and persistent.

Over and above the effects of temporary intoxication, there is also evidence that in a small number of people hallucinogenic drugs and other substances can trigger symptoms of psychotic illness which may persist, and which will need continuing treatment. It is not clear that such drugs are the direct cause, since many people take drugs without going on to develop mental illness. It may be a combination of 'physical vulnerability' (see p. 9) and drug use which lead to mental illness in these cases. Organisations which offer help and support to people with drug-related problems are listed in Chapter 10.

Treatment of organic disorders

- acute symptoms of mental disturbance brought on by physical illness or intoxication may resolve once the underlying physical cause has been treated. More serious symptoms may be treated in their own right, e.g. with antipsychotic drugs

- longer-term organic disorders related to dementia or brain damage are not usually treatable, and the emphasis is focused on helping the person and their family and friends

27

cope with the problems. There are a number of appropriate support groups, e.g. the Alzheimer's Disease Society
(see p. 147)

• **the treatment of addiction and dependency,** which may be
a cause of organic damage, involves the withdrawal of the
alcohol or drugs under close medical supervision, and with
medication to reduce the withdrawal symptoms.
Psychological dependence is also a key factor, and counselling and support are likely to form a crucial part of the
overall treatment. See Chapter 10 for more details and a
list of resources.

• **community care and support** for people with a physical illness or disability are usually organised separately,
although where there are effects on mental functioning
help should also be available from the mental health
services (see Chapter 5)

3

Treatment

**Drugs: effects and side-effects • Electro-convulsive
therapy • Psychosurgery • Psychological therapies •
Complementary therapies • Occupational therapy •
Social care • Consent to treatment**

Modern treatment for mental illness relies heavily on the use
of drugs which are targeted at particular symptoms, and
other forms of treatment and help are sometimes underem-
phasised. It is tempting to imagine that there is a pill for
every ill, but not all problems should be seen as having a
medical cause and solution. For mental health problems to
be properly diagnosed and treated there needs to be an
understanding of the whole person, their social situation and
experience.

However, for serious conditions such as schizophrenia,
manic depression and severe depression, drug treatment is
likely to be a necessary first step. Drug treatment should be
closely supervised, and a brief period of admission to a psychiatric hospital is sometimes advisable. Psychological and
social treatments such as psychotherapy, counselling and
other therapies may also be helpful once the psychotic symptoms have reduced.

Treatment for less serious mental health problems depends
on the nature of the problem, and there is a range of treatments and help available.

29

Being an assertive patient

Medical training enables doctors to look for symptoms, make a diagnosis and prescribe treatment. It does not always equip them to communicate with people in distress, or listen to what they are saying. If you or someone you know are receiving or seeking treatment for mental health problems, make sure that your doctor fully explains the diagnosis, the treatment and its side-effects, and discusses any available alternatives. If the doctor does not volunteer this information, ask for it. Taking control of your own life and taking responsibility for making choices and decisions is part of being mentally healthy; good doctors do not encourage their patients to become passive recipients of treatment.

The stages of successful treatment

- careful assessment of symptoms
- careful assessment of social factors
- accurate diagnosis
- explanation and information
- informed choice of best treatment
- review of treatment
- care and support

DRUGS: EFFECTS AND SIDE-EFFECTS

There are four main types of drugs used in treating mental illness: antipsychotics, mood stabilisers, antidepressants, and anti-anxiety drugs. If you are prescribed any of these drugs, it is important that your doctor gives you information on:

- the effects and purpose of the treatment
- how long it will be before the drug takes effect
- side-effects and what to watch out for
- how long the treatment will be necessary

- any special precautions to be observed in connection with diet, alcohol, pregnancy, breastfeeding and ability to drive

Antipsychotic drugs

Sometimes known as neuroleptics or major tranquillisers, antipsychotic drugs are used in the treatment of schizophrenia, in the manic phase of manic depression, and in other mental disorders where psychotic symptoms occur. They can be very effective in preventing or damping down some of the more distressing symptoms such as delusions and hallucinations. But they do not cure mental illness, and for many people it may be advisable to stay on a maintenance dose of medication long-term, so that their symptoms are controlled and they can continue living a normal life.

The doctor should carefully explain the effects and side-effects of the medication, and try to arrive at the lowest effective dose. As there are many different types of antipsychotic drugs some trial and error may be needed before a doctor finds the drug which suits a particular individual best. These are powerful drugs, and if you are taking them you will need to see your doctor at intervals so that the effects can be discussed and the prescription reviewed if necessary. It may be helpful if you keep a record of dosages and effects.

Antipsychotic drugs are sometimes prescribed in combination with other psychoactive drugs (this is known as polypharmacy); this kind of medication should always be very carefully and expertly monitored. If you have any problems or queries about these drugs it is usually better to discuss them with a consultant psychiatrist, who will have more expertise in this area than a GP.

DEPOT MEDICATION

Antipsychotic drugs can be taken either as tablets, or sometimes in the form of injections. Often known as 'depot' medication, injections have the advantage of being effective for between a week and a month, depending on the drug

31

used. They can be given by a doctor or a nurse at the GP's surgery, at a clinic or at home. This form of treatment can be a helpful alternative if you are forgetful or unreliable about taking tablets.

Antipsychotic drugs

Chemical name	Brand name
Phenothiazines	
Chlorpromazine	Largactil
Thioridazine	Melleril
Trifluoperazine	Stelazine
Fluphenazine*	Modecate
Pipothiazine*	Piportil
Thioxanthenes	
Flupenthixol*	Depixol
Clopenthixol*	Clopixol
Butylperidines	
Haloperiodol*	Serenace/Haldol
Pimozide	Orap
Fluspirilene*	Redeptin
Droperidol	Droleptan
Trifluperidol	Triperidol
Sulpiride	Dolmatil
Risperidone	Risperdal
Clozapine	Clozaryl

Possible side-effects

These may vary according to the individual and the particular drug used. They can include dry mouth, blurred vision, restlessness (akathisia), stiff neck, tremor of hands or feet, menstrual changes, slurred speech, flattening of emotions, sensitivity to sunlight, weight gain, drowsiness and constipation. With Clozapine a reduction in the number of white blood cells occurs, and regular blood tests are essential to monitor this.

*Asterisked drugs are available as slow-release 'depot' injections

SIDE-EFFECTS OF ANTIPSYCHOTIC DRUGS
Antipsychotic drugs are not perfect, and doctors often tend

to play down the unpleasant side-effects. However, this kind of medication can be very effective and it has transformed the treatment of schizophrenia since the introduction of these drugs in the 1950s. Many people who might otherwise have remained in hospital are now able to lead relatively normal lives. As with any treatment, it is a case of weighing the benefits against the risks.

The most common side-effects are shown in the table. Some of them can be controlled by taking other drugs – for example, an anti-Parkinsonian drug called Procyclidine (Kemadrin) is often given to prevent tremor and muscle stiffness which resemble the effects of Parkinson's disease. If side-effects continue to be troublesome, different medication may be tried. Drugs taken by depot injection rather than by tablets can occasionally cause sore lumps near the injection site. This can usually be overcome by changing the medication and/or the injection site.

A more worrying side-effect, because it can be permanent, is **tardive dyskinesia**, in which there are involuntary movements of the face, tongue or body. It is more likely to occur in people who have taken high doses of certain antipsychotic drugs over a number of years. There can also be more serious physical reactions to antipsychotic drugs, although these are fortunately rare.

Some drugs may also **interact with other drugs, alcohol and certain foods.** You should be given information about this by your doctor; if in doubt, ask the doctor or chemist for advice. Some of the interactions can be dangerous, for example people taking antidepressants known as MAOIs (see p. 35) must avoid cheese, yeast/meat extracts and some other foods or their blood pressure may be greatly increased. Full details of foods to be avoided are given on a special card which the chemist will supply together with the prescription.

DOSAGES

Concern has been expressed about some psychiatrists prescribing higher than recommended dosages of these drugs. Detailed information about recommended dosages is available in **The British National Formulary,** published twice a year by the British Medical Association and the Royal Pharmaceutical Society of Great Britain. It can be ordered through bookshops; alternatively, enquire at your local library.

Mood-stabilising drugs

Mood-stabilising drugs

Chemical name	Brand name
Lithium	Priadel, Camcolit
Carbamazepine	Tegretol

Possible Side-effects
These may vary according to the individual and with Lithium may include tremor of the hands and frequent urination; with Carbamazepine, dizziness, nausea and blurred vision.

Lithium (Priadel, Camcolit) can be very effective in the treatment of manic depression. It acts to stabilise mood, and can also be used to control both manic and depressive symptoms. It is essential to have the correct level of Lithium in your blood; if your Lithium levels are too high there can be dangerous physical effects, so doctors always arrange for regular blood tests to be made. People taking Lithium should be given a card by their chemist with advice about precautions. Side-effects can include tremor of the hands and frequent urination.

Carbamazepine (Tegretol), although chemically different from Lithium, is also used to stabilise mood in people with manic depression. It is often used as an alternative treatment when a person has an intolerance to Lithium. It can cause side-effects of dizziness, nausea and blurred vision, particularly when first used.

It may be necessary to continue Lithium or Carbamazepine treatment for months and even years, and to continue taking the drug when in apparent good health in order to prevent a relapse.

Antidepressant drugs

These are used in the treatment of severe or persistent depression, to relieve the symptoms and help to lift mood. They usually take two or three weeks to have an initial effect. Antidepressants are not addictive. They can have side-effects such as causing drowsiness, and some types may produce a reaction with alcohol or with certain foods. The doctor should explain this, and information cards are available. One drawback is that these drugs can be dangerous if taken in overdose, and for this reason doctors are likely to be cautious about prescribing them in quantity for people who may be suicidal.

Depression may, of course, be related to underlying social or psychological problems, and although antidepressant drugs may be helpful they will not resolve such problems. Other kinds of help or treatment such as psychotherapy, or counselling and social support (see Chapter 5) may be more appropriate, or may be combined with drug treatment.

Antidepressant drugs

Chemical name	Brand name	
Tricyclics		
Imipramine	Tofranil	
Amitryptilene	Tryptizol	
Clomipramine	Anafranil	
Dothiepin	Prothiaden	
Doxepin	Sinequan	
Lofepramine	Gamanil	
Related antidepressants		
Mianserin	Bolvidon, Norval	
Maprotiline	Ludiomil	
Trazodone	Molipaxin	
Monoamineoxidase inhibitors (MAOIs)		
Phenelzine	Nardil	
Trancypromine	Parnate	*table continues*

35

Serotonin specific reuptake inhibitors

Fluoxetine	Prozac
Fluvoxamine	Feverin
Paroxetine	Seroxat
Sertraline	Lustral

Possible side-effects

These may vary according to the individual and with tricyclics may include drowsiness, dry mouth, blurred vision, constipation, sweating, behavioural disturbance and occasional heart problems. The related anti-depressants have sedative effects and occasionally give rise to liver and heart problems. MAOIs can produce dangerous interactions with cheese and yeast/meat extracts. The serotonin specific reuptake inhibitors have generally fewer side-effects, which include nausea, vomiting and anxiety.

Anti-anxiety drugs

Also known as minor tranquillisers or anxiolytics, anti-anxiety drugs are sometimes prescribed to reduce anxiety or agitation and to help with sleeping problems. They can be effective for short-term relief of symptoms, but quickly become less effective and can even end up producing the symptoms they are designed to relieve. The major problem is that they can be addictive, and many people have great difficulty coming off them because of their addictive effects and the withdrawal symptoms. For this reason anti-anxiety drugs should only be considered for severe anxiety, and only for a very short period. Other approaches such as counselling and social support are preferable.

Some anti-anxiety drugs are prescribed as sleeping tablets or 'hypnotics'. They are chemically similar to other benzodiazepines, however, and the same drawbacks apply. See p. 159 for details of CITA, an agency with tranquilliser action.

Anti-anxiety drugs

Chemical name	Brand name
Barbiturates	Amytal, Tuinal

Benziodazepines

Chlordiazepoxide	Librium
Diazepam	Valium
Lorazepam	Ativan
Oxazepam	Serenid
Temazepam	Euhypnos
Flurazepam	Dalmane
Nitrazepam	Mogadon
Chlormethiazole	Heminevrin

Beta-blockers

These are used to reduce associated palpitations, sweating, etc, rather than psychological symptoms.

Propranolol	Inderal

Possible side-effects

These may vary according to the individual. Barbiturates may cause dependence and are dangerous in overdose, and for these reasons are now rarely used. Benziodazepines may cause drowsiness, increased anxiety and depression; after a short period they can produce tolerance (the therapeutic effects are reduced), and dependence, so that there are withdrawal symptoms if you stop taking them. Beta-blockers can exacerbate heart problems and asthma.

Abbreviations used in drug treatment

	Latin	Meaning
bd	bis in die	twice a day
tds	ter die sumendum	three times a day
qd	quater in die	four times a day
prn	pro re nata	when necessary
nocte		to be taken at night

ELECTRO-CONVULSIVE THERAPY

ECT is a controversial treatment used mainly in the treatment of severe depression. A course of several ECTs is usually prescribed. Under anaesthetic and with a muscle relaxant, two electrodes are placed on the head and an elec-

37

tric current of about 80 volts is passed through the brain for about half a second. It causes a convulsion and neurochemical effects which are not fully understood. It is common to experience a degree of confusion in the first half-hour after treatment, and some memory disturbance can occur.

While ECT is known to be effective in lifting severe depression in some people, it is often criticised as being a crude and unpleasant treatment, and the opinions of people receiving it are divided. The practice of psychiatrists is also variable – many reserve it as a last resort treatment for extreme depression where, for example, a person has stopped eating or drinking, while other psychiatrists recommend its wider use. It is, however, unlikely to be anyone's first choice.

PSYCHOSURGERY

This means an operation to destroy brain tissue in order to change psychological functioning and influence symptoms. It is used only for a very small number of people – about 25 a year in the UK – who have a long history of very disabling mental illness which has not improved with other treatments; and it is only carried out with their consent. Psychosurgery is both irreversible and hazardous, and remains very controversial.

PSYCHOLOGICAL THERAPIES

Psychological therapies or psychotherapies are talking treatments which can assist with a range of problems such as anxiety, depression and emotional distress. They cannot generally resolve the psychotic symptoms which occur in schizophrenia and manic depression, but may be very helpful as part of follow-up treatment. There are lots of different therapies based on different theories. Some concentrate on the individual while others involve couples or families, or sometimes groups of people in therapy together. There is a distinction between formal psychotherapies and supportive counselling, which is described in Chapter 5.

Psychodynamic psychotherapy

This involves regular meetings with a therapist to explore deep-seated problems and the way they relate to current relationships and early childhood experience. There are various schools of psychodynamic psychotherapy based on the theories of Freud, Jung, Klein and others. The relationship between the patient and the therapist is an important tool in developing insight into problems and finding better ways of coping. This form of psychotherapy usually demands a big investment of time over a long period, and is usually only available privately. It is seldom used in the treatment of serious mental illness because there is no evidence that it is helpful.

Brief psychodynamic therapy

As its name suggests, this is a shorter treatment, which aims to focus on specific problems. The relationship with the therapist is again an important part of the therapy in helping the person to explore feelings, thoughts and behaviour and to see how current problems link with past experiences. Through this process the person is helped to develop insight and the capacity to make changes and resolve problems. This type of therapy can help with a wide range of emotional and psychological problems.

Systemic therapy

This differs from other forms of psychodynamic therapy in that it helps the person to see themselves within the 'system' of relationships of which they are a part, and to understand the roles that they and others have taken on. Through gaining insight into what is going on, you are helped to change old patterns and improve relationships. Other members of the family are likely to be actively involved at some point. **Family therapy** is a form of systemic therapy which is mainly or exclusively carried out with the whole family group. It is often used to help with emotional or behavioural problems experienced by a child or young person within a family. Problems of an individual family member are related to the functioning of the whole family, and the therapy involves improving communications and changing unhelpful patterns of behaviour.

Behavioural therapy

This is a different approach, which concentrates on changing problem behaviour rather than tackling underlying anxieties. Therapists often use a gradual approach which helps people to build up confidence by changing their behaviour in small steps. Behaviour is carefully observed and analysed, to help give an understanding of what may be reinforcing the problem behaviour. Other techniques include rewarding alternative behaviour, learning relaxation to reduce anxiety, and helping people to learn new social skills through practice and role modelling. Therapists usually encourage the person being treated to observe their own behaviour and reassert control over it. This approach can often be most helpful to people who suffer from phobias or obsessive-compulsive disorder, as well as to people who have lost some of their social skills. It is often used together with cognitive therapy.

Cognitive therapy

This aims to help people by altering thinking patterns which may be at the root of their problems. The therapist helps the person to understand and be aware of the thinking processes which are related to their symptoms. Their thinking may have become negative – this can be pointed out, and other ways of seeing things suggested. Cognitive therapy is often used together with behavioural techniques, when it is sometimes called **cognitive-behavioural therapy**. It can be helpful in treating a wide range of problems including anxiety, depression, eating disorders and some of the problems which can occur with serious mental illness.

Other therapies

These include **transactional analysis** in which therapy, often in a group, focuses on 'the child', 'the adult' and 'the parent' as different components of personality. **Gestalt therapy** has an emphasis on the here and now rather than past events; the patient is encouraged to get in touch with aspects of their life and personality which may have been suppressed, so that they can become aware of their needs as a whole person. There are other, less mainstream therapies such as **bioenergetics**, where group therapy concentrates on techniques of breathing, massage and physical touching. **Primal therapy** aims to help people re-experience and resolve traumatic events in very early childhood. **Hypnotherapy** is described on pp. 47–8.

Where to find help

Psychological treatments may be available within the NHS from the clinical psychology department of a psychiatric hospital or through a mental health resource centre if there is one locally. A list of chartered clinical psychologists is available at local libraries. Skilled psychotherapy is an expensive and scarce resource – it may be difficult to obtain, and there is likely to be a waiting list. There is also a national centre for psychotherapy at the Tavistock Centre in London (see below). A referral usually has to be made by a GP or psychiatrist.

Private psychotherapy costs between £20 and £40 per session of one hour. It is very important to choose a therapist who has been properly trained, although sometimes it is possible to see a trainee therapist who is under supervision and charges a reduced fee. Lists are available from the established psychotherapy organisations. Any good therapist will arrange for an assessment first so that an initial understanding of the problems can be reached and an informed decision can be made about the kind of help needed. As long as you are seen by a therapist belonging to a reputable organisation, any problem or complaint you may have regarding your therapy should be dealt with.

Useful addresses

British Association of Psychotherapists
37 Mapesbury Road
London NW2 4HJ
Tel: 0181 452 9823

Can arrange for an initial assessment with experienced therapists in psychoanalytic and analytic psychotherapy. If appropriate, you will then be put in touch with one of their trained members or a trainee receiving supervision. A GP's referral is not necessary. The Association currently has contacts in Brighton, Bristol, Essex, Suffolk, Oxford and York.

British Psychological Society
St Andrews House
48 Princess Road East
Leicester LE1 7DR
Tel: 0116 2549568

The professional body representing psychologists; it keeps a register of all chartered clinical psychologists.

Gestalt Centre
64 Warwick Road
St Albans
Herts AL1 4DL
Tel: 01727 864806

Offers an initial assessment, individual and group work of

a Gestalt orientation in which individuals are encouraged to respond and adapt creatively to life's constant changes. The organisation publishes a nationwide list of Gestalt therapists.

Guildford Centre for Psychotherapy
14 Busbridge Lane
Godalming
Surrey GU7 1PU
Tel: 01483 417443

Offers access to therapists in the southern counties, mainly Surrey, Hampshire and Sussex. Contact them for details and fees.

Guild of Psychotherapists
c/o 19b Thornton Hill
London SW19 4HU
Tel: 0181 947 0730

Offers analytical psychotherapy. An initial consultation costs about £25; fees for regular treatment are negotiable. They also have a low-cost scheme for therapy with trainees, and will advise on therapists throughout Greater London.

Institute of Transactional Analysis
BM Box 4104
Old Gloucester Street
London WC1 3XX
Tel: 0171 404 5011

Produces a list of accredited therapists.

Minster Centre
55 Minster Road
London NW2 3SH
Tel: 0171 435 9200

A training organisation which offers individual and group therapy with a traditional and humanistic orientation. Sessions are available with either qualified or trainee therapists and fees range from £6 to £30 per hour. The Minster Centre also has contacts outside the London area, currently including Bristol, Bath, Taunton, York, Cambridge and Wales.

Tavistock Clinic
120 Belsize Lane
London NW3 5BA
Tel: 0171 535 7111

Offers short-term and long-term individual psychotherapy, and group therapy. It is an NHS service which is available to people in the area and from further afield. Referrals must be made by a GP or other professional. There is an Adult Department, an Adolescent Department and a Child and Family Department.

UK Council for Psychotherapy
Inner Circle
Regent's Park
London NW1 4NS
Tel: 0171 487 7554

Produces a list of accredited psychotherapists, by region. A list of local therapists is available, price £1 per sheet.

COMPLEMENTARY THERAPIES

These therapies are particularly helpful for people experiencing problems with pain control, sleep patterns, anxiety or depression. If you have a serious mental illness you should benefit greatly from the complementary approach where, for example, your anxiety levels are high. However do remember that these therapies are not a substitute for orthodox treatments for acute psychotic symptoms, but complementary to them.

Complementary therapies include:

- acupuncture
- aromatherapy
- herbalism
- homeopathy
- hypnotherapy
- massage
- reflexology
- shiatsu or acupressure

Such natural treatments are also known as 'alternative' therapies; the more up-to-date term, however, is complementary, to stress not only that they can be used alongside conventional treatments, but also that several natural therapies can be used simultaneously. 'Holistic' is another term used to describe many of these therapies and means 'treating the whole person'. Most complementary therapies originated in other cultures, particularly in China and the Indian subcontinent. They are based on entirely different philosophies and approaches to healing from those of orthodox Western medicine.

While there may be disagreement among the medical establishment about the efficacy of complementary therapies, many people do seek help from these treatments and find relief without the side-effects and formality often associated with more conventional medicine. Instead of the emphasis being on diagnosis and chemical treatment, complementary therapies offer a holistic approach where no barriers are maintained between mind, body and spirit. Lifestyle (including diet, smoking, drinking and exercise), attitudes, state of mind, vital energy, posture and the body's natural power to heal itself are all thought to be relevant. The object of many therapies is not just to treat symptoms but also to induce a sense of well-being. The philosophy underpinning the complementary approach is that positive mental health includes feeling empowered enough to make choices and to be in control of your own life.

Complementary therapists usually offer a 45-minute session during which the whole focus is on the client. This contrasts with orthodox medicine where, in the hard-pressed NHS, the GP or psychiatrist is often too busy to give enough time to the whole person or to explain the diagnosis and treatment in detail. Some complementary methods of treatment, such as homeopathy and acupuncture, are increasingly available on the NHS, but such services are patchy and it can still be difficult to find a suitable practitioner. Treatment carried out privately can prove expensive, although some therapists will fit their fees to their client's pocket.

Differences bewtween psychiatric and holistic approaches

Psychiatric approach	Holistic approach
Focus on symptoms and diagnosis, not the person	Focus on the individual and causes of disharmony
Treats symptoms	Treats whole body and psyche
Gives limited information	Shares information more readily
Sees mind and body as separate entities	Mind/body/spirit/emotion wholly integrated
Symptoms seen as illness	Symptoms seen as indication of disharmony
Tries to 'cure' disease	Tries to heal the whole person

Choosing a form of therapy

Before deciding on a complementary therapy, you may wish to consult your doctor to discuss whether your complaint may be best dealt with by conventional medicine. If the latter proves disappointing, the wide range of therapies on offer can make choosing the most effective approach very difficult. Reading about them can provide an overview of the options. Recommendations from friends can help, as can following your own instincts. Some centres offer more than one type of therapy and can advise you on choosing between options (see p. 50 for details of the Natural Health Network). Therapists should tell you if they feel their approach would not be helpful, and may suggest another form of therapy.

The most widely used therapies

Acupuncture belongs to traditional Chinese medicine. It involves using fine needles to stimulate and restore the balance of energy in the body through a series of specific pressure points. Acupuncture is used for a wide range of emotional and physical symptoms, such as digestive problems, migraine, depression and anxiety, and for pain relief.

Aromatherapy uses essential oils which are diluted with water, heated and inhaled, or diluted with base oils and massaged into the body. It is claimed that aromatherapy can help many emotionally based problems.

Herbalism uses plants for healing, to prevent illness and to promote better health. It is the oldest and most widespread system of medicine, and is still a major form of treatment worldwide. Among the plants used for depression are scutellaria (skullcap) and lavender.

Homeopathy is a system of medicine based on the principle of 'like cures like'; that is, an illness can be cured by a substance or drug which produces the same symptoms as the illness itself. Homeopathic remedies are substances diluted so heavily that only a minute trace of them remains. It is claimed that these remedies can stimulate natural healing energy to rebalance the body and return it to health. A substance called Ignatia is used to treat tension, trauma and stress.

Hypnotherapy enables you to attain an altered state of consciousness in which you feel totally relaxed, although still aware of what is being said. It has been described as a natural state similar to daydreaming or being totally absorbed in music. In this state the unconscious mind can be addressed directly and you are much more open to suggestion. Hypnotherapists claim, however, that they cannot make anyone do something they do not want to do.

Hypnotherapy is used to control pain and to treat a number of conditions including tension, stress, anxiety states, insomnia, irritable bowel syndrome, smoking and other addictions. It is very good at assisting deep relaxation and is claimed to increase confidence and the potential to handle problems, but the effects can sometimes be short-lived. Many practitioners feel that people with severe mental health problems such as schizophrenia do not benefit greatly from hypnotherapy and that it is mainly a tool to alleviate the physical symptoms of stress or anxiety. Deep-seated emotional problems are probably better handled by someone trained specifically in psychotherapy or counselling.

Massage is a way of working on the soft tissues, muscles and skin to relieve tension. The chief aim is to promote relaxation, but it can also release physical, mental and emotional blocks. It is useful for combating stress, but it can also bring emotions to the surface.

Meditation has its roots in the contemplative tradition in both Western and Eastern religions. It reduces stress by allowing the person practising it to find inner peace by being still and clearing the mind of thoughts. Meditation is widely taught at evening classes and in many local centres, and can be practised individually for about 20 minutes once or twice daily, or at times of particular stress.

Reflexology is based on the theory that there are invisible lines in the human body along which energy flows. These lines come to the surface in the extremities of the body – the feet, hands and ears. In reflexology, pressure is usually applied to zones in the feet from which pathways run to major organs and other areas of the body. It is a useful diagnostic tool as well as a preventative therapy, and is particulary helpful in relieving tension.

Shiatsu is a massage technique based on promoting health by stimulating energy. Pressure is put on the skin at various points. The word 'shiatsu' means 'finger pressure' and acupressure is a related therapy. This type of technique can be a useful form of self-help therapy.

Finding a therapist

Anyone can set themselves up as a complementary therapist, even if they are untrained or inexperienced, so it is very important to check their credentials. This can be done through the Institute for Complementary Medicine (see below). Many hypnotherapy courses, for example, do not include adequate training in counselling or psychotherapy; the Institute lists only hypnotherapists who work within this framework.

It is often vulnerable people who seek therapy, and unprofessional behaviour such as financial or other exploitation may be encountered. It is wise to agree a contract, including fees, before therapy begins. Some people might also prefer going to a therapist of the same sex as themselves.

Therapists who belong to a professional association have usually received adequate training and will be covered by professional indemnity and public liability insurance. The Institute of Complementary Medicine has compiled a national register for complementary therapies called *The British Register of Complementary Practitioners* which can be obtained from:

Institute for Complementary Medicine
PO Box 194
London SE16 1QZ
Tel: 0171 237 5165

Requirements for membership of the Institute are rigorous.

Because it is the only regulatory body of its kind, and approved by the Department of Trade and Industry, it is likely to become the recognised 'competent authority' for British Complementary Practitioners in line with European standards. The Institute is also working towards setting up a referral service for treatment and training and establishing a common standard of competence and training through the National Council for Vocational Qualifications (NCVQ). Seminars and lectures on holistic health are held by the Institute.

The British Register of Complementary Practitioners currently has 17 divisions covering the following disciplines: aromatherapy; Chinese medicine; colour therapy; counselling; energy medicine; healer counselling; homeopathy; hypnotherapy; massage; nutrition; osteopathy; and reflexology. Lists of practitioners who have reached an agreed standard of competence in their field are available from the Institute.

Other useful addresses

British Holistic Medical Association
179 Gloucester Place
London NW1 6DX
Tel: 0171 262 5299

Aims to educate doctors and the general public in the holistic approach to health. The Association publishes lists of medically qualified practitioners of holistic medicine. It also produces reading lists, a newsletter and self-help cassettes.

Natural Health Network
36a The Tythings
Worcester WR1 1JL
Tel: 01905 619166 or messages can be left on 01905 612521

The Natural Health Network, run on a non-profitmaking basis, has centres across the UK. They provide an information service to the public and offer advice as well as therapies.

OCCUPATIONAL THERAPY

OT can be important in assisting people to get back to normal after a period of mental illness. It concentrates on helping them, both individually and in groups, to regain the skills of daily living – cooking, shopping, self-care, work and leisure skills, and communication. People take part in activities with help and encouragement from the therapist. OT can also help people learn ways of coping with anxiety, depression and lack of confidence, and in this area it overlaps with some kinds of psychotherapy.

Where to find help

Occupational therapists who specialise in mental health problems work in psychiatric hospitals, and OT is usually part of the programme of treatment offered to hospital patients. OTs are also sometimes based in community settings such as day centres.

SOCIAL CARE

This is not 'treatment' in the medical sense, although for many people with a mental illness the distinction between care and treatment is not very meaningful since the one may not be successful without the other. Mental illness in itself causes great stress and distress, but it is also true that some people with a mental illness cope poorly with stress and it can cause them to relapse. The illness can often contribute to a loss of confidence and problems with social relationships. People often have to cope not only with their health problems but also with isolation, housing problems and money worries. It is therefore vital to get advice about managing these difficulties and the stress they cause. Families and carers may also need help and support for themselves.

Where to find help

Assistance and advice should be available from a mental health social worker, a community psychiatric nurse or other advice agencies. See Chapters 4 and 5 for more details.

CONSENT TO TREATMENT

Anyone who is receiving treatment of any kind, whether from a GP or in hospital, should be given **information** to help understand its purpose and effects and any risks. Once you have enough information, you must then give **consent** before treatment can be given. You can withdraw this consent at any time.

However, under common law a doctor may give treatment to someone thought to be **incapable of giving informed consent** – because they are unconscious, for instance, or totally unable to understand. Mental illness does not necessarily mean that a person is incapable of giving consent.

Compulsory treatment may be given without consent under certain circumstances:

- people detained under Sections 2, 3 or 37 of the Mental Health Act may be given drug treatment without their consent for up to three months (see Chapter 7 for details of the various sections of the Act)

- detained patients may be given drug treatment without their consent for longer than three months if a 'second opinion appointed doctor' agrees it is necessary

- electro-convulsive therapy may be given without consent if a 'second opinion doctor' agrees it is necessary

- under Section 62 of the Mental Health Act, **urgent treatment** may be given without consent to any hospital patient in the following circumstances:
  - any treatment may be given in order to save the patient's life

- drug treatment or ECT may be given if necessary to prevent serious deterioration
- non-hazardous drug treatment may be given to alleviate serious suffering or prevent violent or dangerous behaviour. Treatment may be given only for as long as it takes to bring the emergency to an end.

4

Mental Health Professionals

General practitioners • Psychiatrists • Mental health nurses • Community psychiatric nurses • Mental health social workers • Day care and residential workers • Psychologists • Occupational therapists • Other therapists

---

A number of professional groups work with people who have mental health problems – psychiatrists, general practitioners, psychologists, nurses, social workers and various types of therapist. There are differences between what these various professionals do, and in their training and general approach. The different specialist roles can all play a part in helping people, and there is some choice of approaches. But overlaps between their roles can also lead to confusion, especially if everyone concerned is not fully aware of what each other is doing. In order to combat these problems, there is nowadays a growing emphasis on multidisciplinary working, so that all the different mental health professionals work closely together as members of a team.

GENERAL PRACTITIONERS

GPs are often the first point of contact for many people seeking help with a mental health problem, either for themselves or for a member of their family. GPs may have the advantage of knowing their patients and their families well, before mental health problems become apparent. They also keep medical records and can therefore see how current problems relate to past history. Sometimes they are the only professionals involved in the care of a person with a mental health problem; depending on the skills, training and experience of the individual GP, they can play a central role in mental health care.

Minor mental health problems, including depression and anxiety related to stress in relationships or from life events, would be seen by most GPs as part of their normal work. They may, however, refer to other professionals such as psychologists, community psychiatric nurses or mental health social workers for counselling or other help.

With more serious mental illnesses, GPs usually refer patients for specialist assessment to a psychiatrist, who may in turn arrange for hospital treatment. GPs may share outpatient care with the hospital psychiatrist, provide outpatient care themselves, or play only a minimal role. Their main responsibility is to ensure that their patient receives the treatment needed, although GPs may also provide valuable support to the patient and to family members who are also on their practice list. Other professionals such as community nurses and social workers may be involved, in which case the GP would be one of a team providing the care and treatment needed.

How to get help

Everyone has the right to the services of a GP, and most people will already be registered with one. You also have a right to treatment from any GP as a temporary resident while you are away from home for up to three months. If you have any difficulty registering with a GP, contact the local Family Health Service Authority which has lists of GPs and has a duty to allocate you a doctor if necessary. GPs are responsible for the full range of medical problems, and their experience and skills in different specialisms will vary. For this reason it may be worth seeking out a GP who has a particular interest in mental health problems. You could ask people you know if they would recommend a GP, or it might be possible to coax an off-the-record recommendation from a local mental health professional.

PSYCHIATRISTS

A psychiatrist is a doctor who has undergone specific training and specialises in the diagnosis and treatment of people who are mentally ill. Most psychiatrists are based in hospitals, where they are responsible for the care of inpatients and also hold outpatient clinics. In some areas there are community-based mental health centres with a psychiatrist attached. Consultant psychiatrists are the most senior. They may be assisted by a senior registrar or registrar who are also specialists in psychiatry, and by junior doctors who are often known as senior house officers. Of all these doctors it is the junior ones, who are supervised by consultants, who have the most day-to-day contact with patients. However, they usually work at the hospital only on a temporary basis, for a period of three months to a year, as part of their further training. This arrangement means that patients who need ongoing care and treatment may experience a lack of continuity in their relationship with hospital doctors, although the consultant in charge should always have an overview.

Psychiatrists have medical training and are expert in the use of drug treatment, which is the main form of treatment they provide. Some of them also practise psychotherapy, although this is the exception rather than the rule. All psychiatrists work closely with other mental health professionals and may refer to them for other kinds of help. Consultant psychiatrists have ultimate responsibility for the medical care and treatment of their patients, and decide when to admit people to hospital and discharge them.

What happens when you see a psychiatrist?

Appointments with a psychiatrist, particularly in the early stages while they are assessing your problems, usually involve a lot of questions being asked. The psychiatrist will want to hear from you about your current problems and feelings, and will also want to build up a picture of your family life, your occupation and interests, and your social relationships. For a detailed assessment the psychiatrist may carry out a **mental state examination**. He or she will ask questions to test the following areas:

- your mood
- your awareness of time and place, e.g. that you know the day of the week and where you are
- your ability to concentrate, e.g. you may be asked to count backwards from 100, subtracting 7 each time, or to recite the months of the year in reverse order
- memory, both long-term and short-term
- symptoms of mental illness, e.g. whether you have any unusual thoughts or experiences

This process should help the psychiatrist to make a diagnosis of what the problem is, to arrange for further tests if needed, and to decide on the best form of treatment or other help. The psychiatrist may then prescribe treatment, arrange follow-up outpatient appointments or hospital admission if appropriate (see Chapter 6), or may refer back to the GP.

How to get help

The first point of contact is a GP, who can make a referral for an outpatient appointment with a psychiatrist, or can ask one to make a home visit if necessary. Psychiatrists can also be seen privately for a fee, which again is usually via a referral from a GP.

MENTAL HEALTH NURSES

These are nurses who have had special training in psychiatric medicine and have qualified as RMN (Registered Mental Nurse). Their training also provides them with the skills needed to communicate with and support people who are mentally ill. Nurses work closely with the doctors and other professionals and are an important part of the team. They also work with patients in assessing their needs and planning their care, and give medication as directed by a doctor. It is nurses who have the most day-to-day contact with people when they are hospital patients, and most hospitals assign a 'primary nurse' to each patient. A senior nurse (know variously as ward manager, ward sister or charge nurse) usually has overall responsibility for running the ward; sometimes less qualified nurses or nursing auxiliaries help with more basic tasks.

COMMUNITY PSYCHIATRIC NURSES

CPNs are experienced nurses who work with people in the community. They are sometimes referred to as community mental health nurses. CPNs will usually visit you in your own home to provide support, and to advise on various aspects of mental health. Their training enables them to observe the effects and side-effects of medication, and they often give medication as directed by a doctor either in the home or at a hospital or clinic. CPNs work closely with GPs, psychiatrists and other professionals. They have skills in working with people who have emotional or relationship problems, or who suffer from anxiety or stress, for example providing counselling or teaching relaxation techniques. Some CPNs have training in specialist areas, such as eating disorders or behavioural therapy.

How to get help

Referrals to a CPN are usually made by a GP or psychiatrist, though their availability varies widely between one area and the next. CPNs may be involved in supporting people with serious mental illness on a long-term basis.

MENTAL HEALTH SOCIAL WORKERS

These are social workers who have had training and experience in mental health, and are familiar with the problems experienced by users of mental health services and their families. Social workers are employed by the local authority in England, Wales and Scotland (or the Health and Social Services Board in Northern Ireland) and may be based in a local social services office, in a mental health centre or in a hospital. They work closely with other mental health professionals, and in hospitals and mental health centres form part of the multi-disciplinary team. In some areas social workers are still based in non-specialist teams working with a wide range of people (children, elderly people and so on), although this is now increasingly rare as it is recognised that specialist knowledge and skills help social workers to give a better service to people with mental health problems.

Social workers work closely with users and carers in assessing needs, planning care and coordinating help. They have a wider brief than most other mental health professionals and can assist and support people in a range of ways. These may include individual counselling, providing advice to families, and arranging for day care or supported accommodation where necessary. Social workers can also advise and assist people in dealing with other organisations such as the Benefits Agency.

In some areas social workers are known as care managers, although their role does not differ much from that of other social workers. There may also be less highly trained staff who can provide practical help and support.

Approved social workers

ASWs are social workers who have specialist training in making assessments under the Mental Health Act (see Chapter 7 for details). In practice most mental health social workers are also ASWs and undertake this role in addition to the wider one described above. In Scotland social workers undertake a similar role but are known as mental health officers.

How to get help

Social workers can be contacted direct through your local social services office. It is usually possible to make an appointment to see a duty social worker within a few days for an initial discussion or advice. A social worker may then be allocated to work with you, although this priority level of service is usually only available to people with serious problems. In emergencies it should be possible to talk to a social worker without an appointment. Out of office hours, emergency duty social workers can be contacted via the local council; if you have difficulty contacting them, the local police may be able to give you the number.

DAY CARE AND RESIDENTIAL WORKERS

A large number of staff work in day centres and residential homes. Most of them have no formal training; only the more senior staff are likely to have a nursing, social work or occupational therapy qualification. These workers are usually employed by the local social services or by a voluntary agency, although there are some residential homes which are privately run.

Residential and day care workers offer close support to people, both individually and in groups. Each user of the service is usually assigned a link worker or key worker, who is responsible for coordinating the care provided and reviewing it regularly with the user and any other professionals involved, and with carers if appropriate. (See Chapters 5 and

11 for more details about day care and residential care.)

PSYCHOLOGISTS

Clinical psychologists have undergone special training in psychology (the study of human behaviour and the mind) and in mental health, and possess skills in assessing and treating mental illness and psychological problems. Unlike psychiatrists, they are not doctors and they do not prescribe medication. Their skills lie mainly in the assessment of mental health problems and in providing talking treatments such as psychological therapies and counselling. Most psychologists are based in hospitals or in mental health centres, and see people referred to them there by appointment. The type of help they offer depends on the needs of the individual, and they work with the whole range of mental health problems from anxiety through to serious mental illness. The starting point is a thorough assessment, which will involve meeting the psychologist to discuss your problems and whether psychological therapies are likely to be helpful. Psychologists sometimes also carry out psychological tests, usually in the form of a questionnaire, to assist them in making their assessment. Afterwards the psychologist may offer a number of sessions of individual, marital, family or group therapy.

How to get help

Referrals to a psychologist are usually made by a psychiatrist or a GP, who can be asked to arrange a referral. The type of work done by a psychologist is usually one-to-one, which is time-consuming; as a result of this and limited NHS resources they often have quite long waiting lists. (See Chapters 3 and 5 for more details of psychological therapies and counselling.)

OCCUPATIONAL THERAPISTS

OTs are trained to work with people who have a physical or mental disability, to help them regain the skills of daily living. Most psychiatric hospitals have an OT department staffed by therapists who specialise in mental health. People take part in activities, either individually or in groups, with help and support from the therapists, who use daily activities such as cooking, shopping, self-care, work, leisure and artistic skills and communication. OTs may also become involved in counselling people with problems like depression, anxiety, lack of confidence and inability to cope with stress. There can therefore be quite an overlap between their role and that of other mental health professionals such as nurses, social workers, day care workers and psychologists.

How to get help

OTs are usually available to help inpatients in hospital, who are referred by the psychiatrist. There are currently few community-based OTs, but you can ask your GP to refer you to this service if it is available.

OTHER THERAPISTS

A number of other types of therapist also work with people who have mental health problems. These are something of a mixed bag as, unlike most of the professionals described above, there are at the moment no uniform standards of training or accreditation.

Psychotherapists other than trained doctors or psychologists may offer therapy in one of the recognised forms of psychotherapy (see Chapter 3), usually privately. Some schools of therapy demand very long training and rigorous standards of competence before people can practise. It is always wise to check the credentials of anyone offering private therapy: a good therapist will belong to a professional body and will not mind you asking questions.

Counsellors: counselling is a skill which may be used by any of the professionals mentioned in this chapter, or by staff of voluntary organisations. There is currently no agreed standard or qualification for counselling: some counsellors have undergone lengthy training, while others may have had little training but may still be able to offer a useful, though less skilled, service. See pp. 70–84 for more information about counselling and the many organisations which offer this form of help.

Art therapists use art as a means of helping people to communicate and express themselves. This can be a very helpful activity for a wide range of people with mental health problems. Art therapy is widely available in hospital for inpatients or day patients, and also in day centres.

Drama therapists use drama to assist in rebuilding confidence, to help people try out different roles and situations, and sometimes as a means of exploring repressed feelings and anxieties (the latter in particular calls for great skill). It is sometimes available in hospital or in mental health centres.

Complementary therapies: for details of these therapies and advice about finding therapists, see Chapter 3.

5

Care and Support in the Community

There is a wide range of care and support available in the community. The term 'community' is used here, as it often is in mental health services, simply to describe any setting which is not a hospital or closed institution. Community mental health services have developed in a piecemeal way over the years, involving a number of different professionals from the health service, local authorities and voluntary agencies. If you are confused, don't worry – this chapter describes the various kinds of service other than medical treatment that you can expect to find in your locality.

HOW COMMUNITY CARE IS ORGANISED

The NHS and Community Care Act 1990

This important piece of legislation sets out how community care should be provided by health and social services. The philosophy of community care is to provide care to people as far as possible in their own homes rather than in hospitals. One of the main effects of the Act is to make sure that people are offered services which match their needs. This may sound obvious, but in the past people were often offered help according to the services which happened to be available, and were expected to fit in with these rather than the other way round. Greater emphasis is now placed on assessing the individual needs of each person, so that services can be tailored to suit them. Service users and carers are now likely to be asked by their social worker or nurse to complete an assessment form designed to find out about their needs in some detail.

The Act also encourages health and social services authorities to separate the process of assessing need from providing services. The idea is that assessors should be as independent and impartial as possible, so that they are influenced only by the needs of the person. One criticism is that people with mental health problems have very complex needs which vary over time, and so in practice it is the staff who work closely with them and really get to know them who are best able to assess their needs. However, in some areas staff teams have separated into assessors and providers.

Another effect of the Act is that each local authority has to publish and review a community care plan for the local area. This plan should be available at your council offices.

The Care Programme Approach (CPA)

The Care Programme Approach is the title of a government circular sent out in 1990 to all health and local authorities. Its purpose is to prevent people slipping through the net by tightening up the arrangements for providing care to people in need.

The main points of the Care Programme Approach are:

● each person should have an assessment of their needs made

● a care plan should then be agreed and reviewed at intervals

● the philosophy of CPA is that it involves users as fully as possible; users should therefore be involved in meetings and discussions about their care, and should receive a copy of any written care plan

- carers should also be involved in care planning as far as possible, and their contribution should be recognised

- professionals must work together and communicate properly with each other; a care plan can involve a number of different professionals who each have a part to play

- one professional should be nominated as the key worker or care co-ordinator for each person; the key worker, normally a community psychiatric nurse or social worker, is responsible for making sure that the care plan is carried out and reviewed

- a care plan under CPA depends on agreement – it cannot be imposed on someone against their wishes

This policy is supposed to apply to everyone referred to psychiatric services, whatever their problems and needs. One of the difficulties with this is that there are not enough community nurses, social workers or other resources to meet the requirements of everyone. The policy has been interpreted by local health authorities in different ways, and in some areas it is targeted at people who are felt to be most vulnerable or in greatest need.

Community aftercare and the Mental Health Act

The Mental Health Act 1983 has little to say about community care – it is mostly about hospital treatment. However, people who have been on a hospital treatment order under the Mental Health Act (Section 3 or 37) are automatically entitled under Section 117 to aftercare when they leave hospital. There is no compulsion, except that health and local authorities must offer aftercare. In most areas the arrangements are very similar to, or the same as, those for the Care

Programme Approach, with a key worker being nominated and meetings arranged to discuss a care plan.

Guardianship

The other part of the Mental Health Act which deals with care in the community is guardianship under Section 7 (or Section 37 if an order is made by the courts). Guardianship can only be arranged as a result of a formal mental health assessment (see p. 114–15) or through court proceedings. It is a way or providing a framework of authority for a person in the interests of their welfare, or for the protection of others. A guardian is appointed who may be a social worker, or can be a relative. A care plan under guardianship allows the guardian to say where the person should live, and to require them to attend for treatment, occupation, education or training and to give access to certain professionals. There is no authority under guardianship to *give* treatment without consent, only to require the person to attend a particular place.

Supervision registers

From April 1994 a Department of Health circular has required all health authorities to identify people thought to be at significant risk of suicide, or of serious violence to others, or of severe self-neglect. The decision to include a name on the register ultimately rests with the consultant psychiatrist. Supervision registers do not create any new powers or restrictions, and they are a compulsory measure for health authorities rather than for service users. Users must be informed that their name is on the register except where the psychiatrist, in consultation with other professionals involved, considers that informing the user would cause serious harm to his or her physical or mental health. Users cannot prevent their name from being included. Once registered, follow-up under the Care Programme Approach is arranged.

THE RANGE OF CARE AND SUPPORT

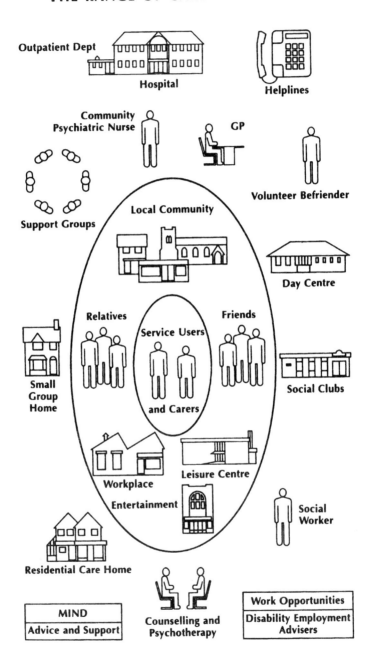

Community mental health centres

The diagram shows the range of help which should be available. In some areas many of these services are grouped together in a single building and referred to as a community mental health centre. The advantages are that mental health professionals are likely to work more effectively together if they are under one roof, they are more likely to be able to offer space for support groups, and it is easier for users to get access to services in one place. If there is no mental health centre in your area, the same services should still be available but will be dispersed in different locations.

How to find the help you need

A good starting point is to find out as much as possible about what is available in your area (see diagram on p. 68). There may be leaflets about local services in your local library, GP's surgery or social services office, and it should always be possible to see one of the mental health professionals mentioned in Chapter 4 and ask for advice. It is usually social workers who know most about the range of local services.

If you feel you have needs which are not being properly met, you can ask the local social services for an assessment. Arrangements vary, and in some areas nurses and other health service staff, as well as local authority staff, carry out assessments of need.

SOCIAL WORK AND COMMUNITY NURSING SUPPORT

Community psychiatric nurses (CPNs) and social workers play a key role in providing care and support to people with mental health problems and their families, in their own homes. Their roles are described in detail in Chapter 4. Because there are only a limited number of staff, it is not possible for everyone with a mental health problem to have

69

their own social worker or CPN. This service is therefore generally limited to people with more serious or persistent problems.

Social workers and CPNs work with their clients to assess their needs and draw up an agreed care plan, which is regularly reviewed. CPNs are medically trained nurses and can administer and monitor medication, whereas social workers' training is more in the areas of social care and emotional problems. Even so, CPNs and social workers often work in a similar way, possess many similar skills, and can help to coordinate help and support. They may work with clients for a short period of a few weeks or months to provide help with a particular problem. Increasingly, however, they are expected to give priority to people who have a serious mental illness and to keep in touch with them on a long-term basis, for instance through fortnightly visits.

Some people will receive help from both a social worker and a CPN if their circumstances call for it. However, depending on the local arrangements it is more likely that one or other professional will act as a continuing key worker or coordinator who can bring in other help for brief periods when it is needed.

How to get help

Social workers can be contacted direct through the local social services office, or at a community mental health centre if there is one in your area. CPNs can also be contacted through a community mental health centre, otherwise through a referral from a GP or psychiatrist.

COUNSELLING AND OTHER FORMS OF HELP

Counselling is a form of one-to-one talking treatment which is less formal than psychotherapy (see Chapter 3). Counsellors usually try to help the person focus on particular difficulties at a practical and immediate level. They offer advice on how best to tackle those problems which can be solved, and how to come to terms with those which cannot. An alternative to individual counselling is group work, where problems are shared with people in the same boat, the relationship with the group leader is not so intensive and sessions are often cheaper.

Free counselling or groupwork may be available from community psychiatric nurses or social workers (see pp. 58–59). National and regional MIND offices (see p. 91–93) will also be able to provide information on help available in specific areas of the country. The organisations listed below are examples of the main sources of counselling and other help available, or those that cover a wider than local area, and they will point people towards the support they need. Make sure that counsellors are properly qualified and any fees explained before you start. Where helplines are available, details have been included. Assistance for specific groups such as elderly people, people with addiction and dependency problems, women, people from ethnic minorities, children and young people and carers can also be found in Chapter 10.

General help (counselling and self-help)

British Association for Counselling (BAC)
1 Regent Place
Rugby
Warwickshire CV21 2PJ
Tel: 01788 578328

BAC does not provide counselling but is an umbrella organisation. It has developed a code of ethics for counsellors and operates an accreditation scheme for courses and individuals. It also produces a range of information sheets about the nature of counselling and what particular types of counselling are available. A guide on how to approach a counsellor, and lists of counselling organisations and individual counsellors in local areas, are also available.

Cambridge Group Work
4 George Street
Cambridge CB4 1AJ
Tel: 01223 64543

Provides details of small therapy groups and opportunities for training in group work, mainly in East Anglia and covering a range of needs. Referral can be made by GPs, psychiatrists or the person themselves. Details of fees etc. are available from the administrator.

Depressives Anonymous
36 Chestnut Avenue
Beverley
North Humberside HU17 9QU
Tel: 01482 860619

Provides information about local self-help groups nationwide. Also runs a penfriend scheme, provides information and support for depressives, produces a quarterly newsletter and maintains a booklist.

Depressives Associated
PO Box 1022
London SE1 7QB
Tel: 0181 760 0544 (ansaphone)

Run by ex-depressives who aim to inform and educate people about this illness and provide encouragement for sufferers and their families. They also help those who are depressed by putting sufferers in touch with each other via a penfriend scheme, help members form self-help groups in order to encourage mutual support, and produce a quarterly newsletter.

Isis Centre
Little Clarendon Street
Oxford OX1 2HS
Tel: 01865 56648

Provides NHS counselling and psychotherapy for individuals, couples, families and groups. This is a self-referral service for people who live in Oxfordshire, and there are no fees.

Samaritans
10 The Grove
Slough
Berkshire SL1 1QP
Tel: 01753 532713 (administration). Local numbers are listed under 'S' in telephone directories and on the inside front covers of most.

A national organisation covering England, Ireland, Scotland and Wales, with over 185 branches open 24 hours every day of the year. They offer confidential support to those in distress who feel suicidal or despairing.

Seasonal Affective Disorder Association (SADA)
PO Box 989
London SW7 2PZ
Tel: 0181 969 7028

Seasonal affective disorder (SAD) is a regularly recurring winter depression which affects some people every year between October and April. SADA is a self-help organisation which gives advice and support to sufferers and a limited phone counselling service. An information pack, including details of light therapy, is available to enquirers.

Westminster Pastoral Foundation
23 Kensington Square
London W8 5HN
Tel: 0171 937 6956

Centres in London and throughout the UK offer a range of counselling services including individual, couple, family and group therapy as well as counselling for the physically ill and a young persons' service. Sessions are available with both qualified therapists and trainees. Fees vary according to means, but usually range between £5 and £30 per individual session.

Help with anxiety

First Steps to Freedom
22 Randall Road
Kenilworth
Warwickshire CV8 1JY
Tel: 01926 851608 (helplines open 10am–10pm daily)

Offers help to those who suffer from general anxiety, phobias, obsessive compulsive disorders (checking, washing, fear of contamination etc.). They produce a wide range of leaflets and audiotapes.

Obsessive Action
c/o Dr S. A. Montgomery
Paterson Wing
St Mary's Hospital
Paddington
London W2 1NY

A newly formed self-help association set up by a group of fellow sufferers and their doctors to promote awareness, recognition and treatment of obsessive compulsive disorder (OCD). Information is provided to sufferers, their relatives, friends and anyone else with an interest. They can supply details of any self-help support groups that may be available, as well as a regular members' newsletter.

Phobic Action
Hornbeam House
Claybury Grounds
Manor Road
Woodford Green
Essex IG8 8PR
Tel: 0181 559 2551 (administration) Helplines 0181 559 2459 (London) and 01452 856021 (Gloucester) 10am–10pm every day of the year

A national organisation offering support to sufferers of anxiety problems, including panic attacks, phobias or obsessional compulsive disorders, and to their families. They have a network of local self-help recovery groups, some of which offer home visits. The helpline numbers contain a recorded message giving the phone numbers of volunteers on call.

Action on Phobias (Scotland)
see p. 243

Northern Ireland Agoraphobia and Anxiety Society
See p. 244

Phobics Society
See p. 245

Relaxation for Living Trust
168–170 Oatlands Drive
Weybridge
Surrey KT13 9ET
Tel: 01932 831000

Produces books and cassettes which help with relaxation, panic attacks and phobias. They produce leaflets and a national list of people who teach relaxation classes, and also train people to teach relaxation.

Help with eating disorders

Anorexia and Bulimia Care (Southern)
Arisaig
Back Lane
Monks Eleigh
Suffolk IP7 7BA
Tel: 01449 740145

Anorexia and Bulimia Care (Northern)
15 Fernhurst Gate
Aughton
Ormskirk
Lancashire L39 5ED
Tel: 01695 422479

The northern office covers the area north of a line from the Bristol Channel to the Wash, while the Southern office covers the area south of that line. They offer help, support and information from a Christian perspective to sufferers and their carers.

Eating Disorders Association
Sackville Place
44–48 Magdalen Street
Norwich
Norfolk NR3 1JU
Tel: 01603 619090 (administration and general information 9–5pm). Helpline 01603 621414 (Monday–Friday 9–6.30pm with ansaphone service out of hours). Youth helpline 01603 765050 (Monday, Tuesday and Wednesday 4–6pm)

Supports and advises sufferers of anorexia and bulimia nervosa, also their families and friends. They offer a network of self-help groups and contact addresses, issue a newsletter every two months and run a book and mailing service.

Help with bereavement and loss

Compassionate Friends
53 North Street
Bristol BS3 1EN
Tel: 0117 0665202 (administration). Helpline 0117 9539639 (9.30–5pm. An ansaphone message outside these hours will give alternative numbers.)

Nationwide self-help organisation of bereaved parents offering support and friendship to newly bereaved parents whose child, of any age, has died from any cause. They also pro-

76

duce a range of leaflets and a quarterly newsletter and have a postal library for members.

CRUSE – Bereavement Care
Cruse House
126 Sheen Road
Richmond
Surrey TW9 1UR
Tel: 0181 940 4818 (general). Helpline 0181 332 7227
(Monday–Friday 9.30am–5pm.)

Has over 190 local branches covering the whole of the UK. They offer counselling, practical advice, encouragement and opportunities for social support to all bereaved people, as well as publishing a wide range of literature.

Foundation for the Study of Infant Deaths
35 Belgrave Square
London SW1X 8QB
Tel: 0171 235 0965

Provides advice and counselling for newly bereaved parents after sudden infant death ('cot death'). There is a network of over 140 local groups as well as an individual befriending service, a newsletter and information leaflets.

Lesbian and Gay Bereavement Project
Vaughan M. Williams Centre
Colindale Hospital
Colindale Avenue
London NW9 5HG
Tel: 0181 200 0511 (administration). Helpline 0181 455 8894
(24-hour ansaphone giving name and phone number of volunteer on call that evening between 7pm and midnight.

Helps and supports lesbians and gay men bereaved by the death of their partner or otherwise affected by a bereavement. They can also help with will forms and funeral arrangements.

National Association of Bereavement Services
20 Norton Folgate
London E1 6DB
Tel: 0171 247 0617

Provides information on local bereavement counselling services and advice about the most appropriate service.

Stillbirth and Neonatal Death Society (SANDS)
28 Portland Place
London W1N 4DE
Tel: 0171 436 5881

Offers advice and long-term support to newly bereaved parents (from 22 weeks of pregnancy to one or two months after birth) through a network of over 200 local self-help groups and contacts. Also provides information, leaflets and a newsletter.

Help with relationships

Family Mediation Scotland
127 Rose Street
South Lane
Edinburgh EH2 5BB
Tel: 0131 220 1610

The contact address for services in Scotland provided by the National Association of Family Mediation and Conciliation Services (see below).

Institute of Family Therapy
43 New Cavendish Street
London W1M 7RG
Tel: 0171 935 1651

Provides couple and family therapy plus a mediation service for couples divorcing and/or separating. Self-referral is possible, as is referral through health, education or social services departments. There is a sliding scale of fees according to the total family or couple's income; if the total income is less than £10,000 no fee is charged. The service is available to anyone in the UK and the Institute also has a limited register of family therapists outside London.

Marriage Counselling Scotland
105 Hanover Street
Edinburgh EH2 1DJ
Tel: 0131 225 5006

A voluntary, confidential counselling service at 15 local centres for couples and others in intimate personal relationships.

National Association of Family Mediation and Conciliation Services
Charitybase
The Chandlery
50 Westminster Bridge Road
London SE1 7QY
Tel: 0171 721 7658

There are over 60 out-of-court mediation services in England, Wales and Northern Ireland linked to this Association. The help offered is aimed at couples who are or are about to become separated or divorced, and are having disagreements over important issues, especially those concerning their children. There are no set fees but a sliding scale, based on ability to pay, is operated by some services.

Parents Anonymous
Manor Gardens Centre
6–9 Manor Gardens
London N7 6LA
Tel: 0171 263 8918 (helpline giving recorded message with name and number of volunteer on call that evening 7pm–midnight)

For parents who feel they cannot cope or who feel that they might abuse their children.

RELATE (formerly Marriage Guidance Council)
Herbert Grey College
Little Church Street
Rugby
Warwickshire CV21 3AP
Tel: 01788 573241 (ring this number for details of your
regional office)

Coordinates about 130 local RELATE Centres in England, Wales and Northern Ireland offering counselling to people who have problems with their personal relationships. Sexual therapy and a family mediation service are also available. RELATE is a charitable organisation and a sessional donation is discussed at the first appointment, though no one is denied help through lack of money. People should be prepared to wait for an appointment.

Sex and sexuality

Albany Trust Counselling
Sunra Centre
26 Balham Hill
London SW12 9EB
Tel: 0181 675 6669

Offers confidential psychotherapy and counselling for all types of sexual identity, psychosexual and relationship problems, plus telephone advice. The counselling service covers the Greater London areas and parts of Sussex, Kent and Hertfordshire. The fees are £30 for individuals and £40 for couples per session. Concessions can be arranged for people on benefit or a low income.

Beaumont Trust
BM Charity
London WC1N 3XX
Tel: 0171 730 7453 (helpline Tuesday 7–11pm for
transvestites, Thursday 7–11pm for trans-sexuals); 0606
871984 (Monday evening helpline for partners)

Offers information and a confidential befriending service and helpline for people with gender dysphoria, transvestites and trans-sexuals.

Black Lesbian and Gay Centre
Arch 196
Bellenden Road
London SE15 4RF
Tel: 0171 732 3885

Offers advice, information and support to black lesbians and gay men. This is a London-wide service, but advice is given to all callers.

Gender Dysphoria Trust International
Archer House
Britland Estate
Northbourne Road
Eastbourne
Sussex BN22 8PW
Tel: 01323 641100

Provides information, counselling and literature for trans-sexuals and those caring for them. Also has a helpline service, a bi-monthly journal and ongoing support groups, and offers medical information on gender reassignment and legal help and advice. Normally fees for counselling are determined on an individual basis, but the standard charge is currently £35. See also Partners Group below.

Lesbian and Gay Switchboard
BM Switchboard
London WC1N 3XX
Tel: 0171 837 7324 (24-hour helpline)

Information service to lesbians and gay men.

Manchester Gay Centre
PO Box 153
Manchester M60 1LP
Tel: 0161 274 3814. The Manchester Lesbian and Gay
Switchboard is also at this address: 0161 274 3999 every day
4–10pm.

Offers a safe, confidential advice and information service to
the gay and lesbian, bisexual, transvestite and trans-sexual
communities in the north-west of England.

PACE
34 Hartham Road
London N7 9JL
Tel: 0171 700 1323

Specialises in counselling for lesbians, gay men and people
unsure of their sexuality. They provide crisis counselling of
up to three sessions, short-term counselling of up to 12 sessions and some longer-term counselling. Fees are on a sliding
scale depending on income, and languages other than
English are usually available.

Partners Group
BM Box 7624
London WC1N 3XX
Tel: 01323 641100

For partners and families of trans-sexuals. Part of the Gender
Dysphoria Trust International (see above).

HIV and AIDS counselling

Black HIV/AIDS Network (BHAN)
1st Floor
St Stephen's House
41 Uxbridge Road
London W12 8LH
Tel: 0181 749 2828

BHAN incorporates the Asian AIDS Project (AAP) and is a national organisation for Asian, African and Afro-Caribbean communities. It provides counselling, community services, support and information to black and Asian people living with HIV or AIDS, and to their families, carers and partners.

Blackliners
Eurolink Centre
49 Effra Road
London SW2 1BZ
Tel: 0171 738 7468 (administration). Helpline 0171 738 5274
(Monday–Friday 10–8pm, Saturday 1–6pm.)

Produce and distribute information about HIV and AIDS aimed at the Asian, African and Afro-Caribbean communities. They also provide counselling, advocacy and housing for black and Asian people affected by HIV and AIDS as well as care, practical and emotional support to families, carers, dependants and partners.

Mainliners
205 Stockwell Road
London SW9 9SL
Tel: 0171 737 7472 (administration). Helpline 0171 737 3141
(Monday–Wednesday 11–4pm, Thursday 11–8pm, Friday 11–3pm.)

National telephone helpline for people worried about HIV infection or AIDS connected to drug abuse. There is also a drop-in clinic at the above times which offers support and advice to drug users and ex-users.

National AIDS Helpline
PO Box 1577
London NW1 3DW
Tel: 01800 567123 (24 hours), 01800 282446 Tuesday
6–10pm (Cantonese and English), 01800 282445 Wednesday
6–10pm (Bengali, Gujerati, Hindi, Punjabi, Urdu and

English), 01800 282447 Wednesdays 6–10pm (Arabic and English); mini-com line for those hard of hearing: 01800 521361 daily 10am–10pm.

National free phone line offering confidential advice and information or referral on any aspect of HIV and AIDS to anyone. Also has details of local groups and agencies.

Terrence Higgins Trust
52–54 Grays Inn Road
London WC1X 8JU
Tel: 0171 831 0330. Helpline 0171 242 1010 (daily 12 noon–10pm.) Legal line 0171 405 2381 (Wednesdays 7–10pm.)

Offers advice and information on housing, welfare and legal matters. Also runs support services such as the Buddy Scheme, which offers individual befriending to people living with AIDS. Telephone counselling is available on the helpline number to people who are HIV positive or have AIDS, and to their families. Details of local groups and projects are also available.

DAY CARE

Most people need to occupy their time during the day, particularly if they have a mental health problem. The aim of day care is to provide recreation, therapy and rehabilitation, and the company and support that are offered can ease the loneliness and isolation that often go hand in hand with mental illness. Day care is usually provided in centres run by social services or voluntary agencies such as MIND. It may also be provided as one of the services in a community mental health centre as mentioned on p. 69.

Staff help to organise activities such as discussion groups and anxiety management groups, keep fit, yoga, art, cookery and woodwork. In many day care centres each user has a link worker or key worker assigned to them. This worker will discuss your particular needs and interests and arrange a programme accordingly; they may also be able to offer informal counselling. The programmes offered may involve attending for particular groups and activities for anything from one morning or afternoon session to five full days a week.

Drop-in centres and social clubs

Most areas have informal drop-in centres or social clubs where people can meet others who are in the same situation and enjoy each other's company in a relaxed atmosphere. There may be one or two staff or volunteers on hand, and leisure facilities such as board games, table tennis and snooker. This can be a very good way of keeping in touch with other people when more formal therapeutic activities are either not needed, not suitable or unavailable.

Weekends and evenings are often the times when people most want social and recreational facilities, and an increasing number of drop-ins and social clubs now have opening hours to reflect this need.

HOW TO APPLY

Contact your local social services, MIND office or any of the mental health professionals mentioned in Chapter 4 for details of day care services in your area and how to gain acces to them.

BEFRIENDING

We all need friends to chat with, go out with or turn to for practical help, and yet people with mental health problems often lack the confidence to make friends and so find themselves becoming lonely and isolated. Others may have lost their friends because of their illness; perhaps they went through a period of acting irrationally, or withdrew from social contact. But nowadays there is a growing number of befriending schemes throughout the country, run by local voluntary organisations such as MIND or by social services.

Such schemes help by putting people in touch with volunteer befrienders, who are able to share a different kind of relationship with people than the more formal relationships offered by professionals. Befrienders are usually given training and then carefully matched with their friend, to whom they offer support and friendship on a one-to-one basis. Once matched, volunteer befrienders are given regular supervision and support. Your local social services department or regional MIND office (see p. 92) should know if there is a scheme in your area.

SELF-HELP THROUGH THE USER MOVEMENT

The limitations of professional support

People who have mental health problems very often say that what they value most is the support and companionship of other people in the same situation. Fellow users have a personal experience which even the best trained and most skilful professionals lack. Professionals are often committed and dedicated, but ultimately they are paid for what they do and go home at the end of the day, which limits the sort of relationship they can offer. Self-help user groups do not suffer from these inevitable shortcomings.

In the past mental health professionals assumed the role of the expert and told their patients what to do, encouraging them to be passive and excluding them from any discussion about their care and treatment. But in recent years doctors, nurses, social workers and others have started to follow a new philosophy of working in partnership with service users, as already mentioned. Nevertheless some professionals have been slow to adapt. If this is your experience, you may find that one of the self-help organisations listed below can assist you. Chapter 11 explains your rights and how to complain if this becomes necessary.

The user movement

In many areas there are now user groups which are independent of professionals and which act both as pressure groups to promote change and better services, and also as a valuable source of mutual support. As a result users are now much more frequently consulted about local services than they used to be. Becoming involved in a user group is about taking power, saying what you want and asserting your rights. To find out if there is a user group in your area contact your local branch of MIND or one of the following organisations:

Good Practice in Mental Health (GPMH)
380–384 Harrow Road
London W9 2HU
Tel: 0171 289 2034

A national voluntary organisation with experience in supporting and advising user groups

Hearing Voices Network
Fourways House
1st Floor
16 Tariff Street
Manchester M1 2EP
Tel: 0161 228 3896

The Hearing Voices Network is a user-led project that aims to help people cope and live with their voices. The above number will give details of local groups and about assistance in forming new groups.

MINDLINK (the MIND consumer network)
Granta House
15–19 Broadway
London E15 4BQ
Tel: 0181 519 2122

MINDLINK is open to everyone who has had psychiatric

treatment in hospital or in the community. It is a contact and advisory network which enables MIND to benefit from service users' experiences. Through its information service and contact list MINDLINK helps to strengthen the growing voice of patients and ex-patients of the psychiatric services. MINDLINK also aims to reflect our multi-racial society by bringing together people from different races and cultures. It challenges the racism, sexism and other forms of oppression that are the cause of so much emotional distress in our society. Members receive the regular newsletter *Mindwaves*.

Survivors Speak Out
34 Osnaburgh Street
London NW1 3ND
Tel: 0171 916 5472

A national users' organisation to which a number of local groups and individuals are affiliated. Its activities include support, campaigning, training, networking and an information service. It also produces a newsletter and other publications of particular importance to survivors of the mental health system.

UK Advocacy Network (UKAN)
Premier House
14 Cross Burgess Street
Sheffield S1 2HG
Tel: 01742 753131

A federation of patients' councils, user forums and advocacy projects, all of which are led by users or ex-users of mental health services. They can supply details of local groups.

VOICES Forum
c/o NSF National Office
28 Castle Street
Kingston-upon-Thames
Surrey KT1 1SS
Tel: 0181 547 3937

A network of local groups run by and for people who have first-hand experience of serious mental health problems. The above phone number will give you a local contact.

ADVICE AND INFORMATION

A lot of ignorance and fear still surrounds mental health issues; it can damage users and ex-users of mental health services and it can bewilder carers. Knowledge will give you confidence and enable you to ask the right questions. Mental health professionals should be able to give advice and information about mental health and local services. Listed below are agencies which offer advice and information on mental health issues. Chapter 10 offers more specialised advice.

Association of Community Health Councils for England & Wales (ACHCEW)
30 Drayton Park
London N5 1PB
Tel: 0171 609 8405

ACHCEW runs an advisory and information service for the over 200 Community Health Councils (CHCs) in England and Wales, and represents health service users at a national level. The address of your local CHC can be found in your local library, telephone directory or Citizens' Advice Bureau; alternatively, contact ACHCEW.

A typical CHC provides advice and information about national health services and acts as a consumer watchdog of the NHS by monitoring local services, surveying local need and recommending improvements to the local health authority/health agency.

CHCs can also give advice on patients' rights and how to complain, details of specialist help, and special assistance such as translating.

Details of the 22 **Welsh CHCs** can also be obtained from:

Association of Welsh CHCs
c/o East Glamorgan CHC
13 Gelliwastad Road
Pontypridd
Mid Glamorgan CF37 2BW
Tel: 01443 405830

For **Scotland,** contact:

Scottish Association of Health Councils (SAHC)
5 Leamington Terrace
Edinburgh EH10 4JW
Tel: 0131 229 2344

The umbrella organisation for Scotland's 18 Local Health Councils, which provides much the same service as ACHCEW.

In **Northern Ireland** there are four Health and Social Services Councils, which provide a similar service to England's CHCs:

Southern Health and Social Services Council
16 Church Street
Portadown
Co. Armagh BT62 3LQ
Tel: 01762 351165

Western Health and Social Services Council
Hilltop
Tyrone and Fermanagh Hospital
Omagh BT79 0NS
Tel: 01662 245828

Eastern Health and Social Services Council
19 Bedford Street
Belfast BT2 7EJ
Tel:01232 321230

Northern Health and Social Services Council
8 Broadway Avenue
Ballymena
Co. Antrim BT43 7AA
Tel: 01266 655777

Federation of Independent Advice Centres (FIAC)
13 Stockwell Road
London SW9 9AU
Tel: 0171 274 1839

An umbrella organisation whose 800+ members are all independent agencies that give free advice as part of their work. They provide training and a publications list, and can help people get in touch with their local advice centre.

MIND (National Association for Mental Health)
Granta House
15–19 Broadway
London E15 4BQ
Tel: 0181 519 2122 (general office line, also contact number for legal advice line open Monday, Wednesday and Friday 2–4.30pm.) Information line 0181 522 1728 (Monday–Friday 10am–12.30pm and 2–4.30pm.)

MIND is the leading mental health charity in England and Wales. It works for a better life for people diagnosed, labelled or treated as mentally ill and campaigns for their right to lead an active and valued life in the community. In all its activities MIND stresses the particular needs of black people, women and other oppressed groups.

Since its launch in 1946, MIND has grown into a movement with a solid network of supporters and local associations throughout England and Wales. Drawing on the knowledge and skills of people who both provide and use mental health services, MIND has established itself not only as the largest independent provider of care in the community, but also as an influential commentator on government policy in all areas of mental health.

MIND has over 240 local associations which rely on paid staff as well as the enthusiasm and energy of volunteer workers. Local MIND groups are involved in a range of activities from counselling to relatives' support schemes; employment projects to supported housing; befriending schemes to drop-in centres. For details of local MIND projects and other options available to people with mental health problems and their families and friends, contact your regional office:

North West MIND
21 Ribblesdale Place
Preston PR1 3NA
Tel: 01772 821734

Northern MIND
158 Durham Road
Gateshead NE8 4EL
Tel: 0191 490 0109

South West MIND
9th Floor, Tower House
Fairfax Street
Bristol BS1 3BN
Tel: 0117 9250960

Trent and Yorkshire MIND
The White Building
Fitzalan Square
Sheffield S1 2AY
Tel: 01742 721742

West Midlands MIND
20–21 Cleveland Street
Wolverhampton WV1 3HT
Tel: 01902 24404

MIND South East
1st Floor, Kemp House
152–160 City Road
London EC1V 2NP
Tel: 0171 608 0881

Wales MIND
23 St Mary Street
Cardiff CF1 2AA
Tel: 01222 395123

MIND Mail Order Service
Granta House
15–19 Broadway
London E15 4BQ
Tel: 0181 519 2122

Contact MIND Mail Order for their list and order form, which covers a wide range of publications and leading titles in the field of mental health. Included are MIND's *Understanding* series of advice leaflets, which give straightforward, practical information on a range of mental health conditions and issues. Each leaflet offers realistic, positive advice and contains a resource list for seeking further help.

MIND believes that people have a right and responsibility to give informed consent to treatment. Its two series *Special Reports* and *Making Sense of Treatments and Drugs* give people the information they need about various treatments, including their effects and unwanted side-effects.

Northern Ireland Association for Mental Health
80 University Street
Belfast BT7 1HE
Tel: 01232 328474

A charity which promotes dignity, choice, integration and participation for those with mental health needs, the Association offers advice and information on mental health issues. It also has a network of Beacon Centres throughout the province which offer a wide range of services including individual programmes of day care, recreational and therapeutic activities, advocacy and home care schemes. There are also Beacon House Clubs and residential schemes, details of which are available from the above address.

SANE
199–204 Old Marylebone Road
London NW1 5QP
Tel: 0171 724 6520. Saneline (helpline) 0345 67 8000 (calls charged at local rate); 0171 724 8000 (if calling from London) every day of the year, including weekends and bank holidays, 2pm– midnight.

A national charity set up to raise awareness of serious mental illness and fund research into causes and possible cures. It is a campaigning organisation and is keen to hear from people who wish to speak out about their experiences. SANE has a legal department and tries to get help for those who need it – suggesting friendly lawyers and courses of action. It also provides care projects such as Saneline, which gives confidential support, information and help to people with mental health problems and their carers. SANELINE staff are trained volunteers and have access to information about resources throughout the UK. (SANELINE always needs more volunteers – if you would like to be a volunteer, contact SANELINE administration on 0171 724 6750.)

Scottish Association for Mental Health (SAMH)
Atlantic House
38 Gardner's Crescent
Edinburgh EH3 8DQ
Tel: 0131 229 9687

A voluntary organisation which provides direct services to people with mental health problems in Scotland and campaigns for their fundamental human and citizen's rights. Among the services provided are information; a range of accommodation depending on the level of support needed; an outreach service which includes domiciliary support to enable people to continue living in their own homes or to support people returning home after a spell in hospital; and a respite care facility intended to prevent relapse, to give carers a break or to provide an alternative to hospital admission and training and employment projects. There are four regional offices:

South and East Region SAMH
17a Graham Street
Edinburgh EH6 5QN
Tel: 0131 555 5959

North Region SAMH
Harbour Buildings
Ferryden
Montrose DD10 9SL
Tel: 01674 77899

West Region SAMH
Maritime House
246 Clyde Street
Glasgow G1 4JN
Tel: 0141 248 8558

Forth Valley and Fife Region SAMH
Haypark Business Centre
Marchmont Avenue
Polmont
Falkirk FK2 0NZ
Tel: 01324 717892

National Schizophrenia Fellowship
NSF National Office
28 Castle Street
Kington Upon Thames
Surrey KT7 1SS
Tel: 0181 547 3937 (General Office); 0181 974 6814 (advice line Monday–Friday, 10am–3pm).

A national voluntary organisation which supports men and women with a severe mental illness, their families and carers. They are a campaigning organisation and have a large network of over 150 local groups. For a fuller description of NSF's activities and the addresses of regional offices, see p. 140–1.

Making Space
46 Allen Street
Warrington
Cheshire WA2 7JB
Tel: 0925 571680
(Covers North West England)

Making Space
111a Otley Road
Headingly
Leeds LS6 3PX
Tel: 0532 746010
(Covers West Yorkshire)

Making Space offers a service of help and support to people in the North of England affected by the problem of Schizophrenia. They also promote and manage facilities such as day centres, employment schemes and a range of supported housing for different needs. They have over 40 self-help groups for sufferers and their relatives and also organise seminars and conferences to further the understanding of schizophrenia and its consequences. Please contact either of the above numbers for details of local schemes and services.

6

Hospital Care

The last few decades have seen tremendous changes in the treatment and philosophy of care for mentally ill people, with a move away from institutional care and its emphasis on custody and containment. Many people lived for very long periods in these old institutions; standards of care could be poor and patients were sometimes abused and neglected. In this situation people easily became submissive and apathetic, and as a result grew permanently dependent on the institution.

More humane attitudes and improvements in medical treatment have led to the closure of many of the old-style Victorian mental hospitals. Today the arrangements for people who need such medical care and treatment vary across the country. Some areas still rely on the remaining facilities in old-style mental hospitals, but in general there has been a shift to providing treatment in psychiatric or mental health units which are part of district general hospitals.

AIMS OF HOSPITAL CARE

The emphasis in today's mental health hospitals is on **treatment,** and people stay in hospital no longer than necessary. Most hospitals rely heavily on medication. Modern

96

psychiatric drugs, first developed in the 1950s, enable many people with a serious mental illness to lead independent lives, where previously they would have needed long-term care and support.

Mental health hospitals also have a role in providing **rehabilitation** and **continuing care** for people who need longer-term facilities. Rehabilitation, which means 'restoring to full ability and health', involves assisting people to learn or relearn the skills of daily life and of social relationships. It enables them to move out of hospital into independent housing or, if necessary, supported accommodation (see Chapter 12). For a very small number of people who need more support or supervision than is available in their own community, continuing care in hospital can be provided.

Outpatient care

Mental health services are becoming less hospital-based. The traditional system of outpatient hospital care is giving way in some areas to support from teams of mental health professionals based in mental health centres outside hospitals (see Chapter 4 for details of community-based care). However, in most areas outpatient care is still offered from the local mental health unit attached to the district general hospital.

Outpatient appointments

An initial appointment with a psychiatrist at the outpatient clinic is usually arranged by a GP. On this occasion you are likely to see a consultant psychiatrist or registrar, who will discuss your problems and decide on the appropriate treatment or help (see also p. 56). This may include prescribing medication or making a referral to a psychologist, a community psychiatric nurse or other professionals. If you have further outpatient appointments it is likely that you will be seen by a junior doctor under the supervision of the consultant. In most hospitals the juniors are only on temporary contracts, so you probably won't see the same doctor at each appointment throughout a course of treatment. Some people find this lack of continuity unsettling, although all the doctors whom you see will have read your medical notes.

Day hospital care

Day care is provided in many hospitals, although increasingly the trend is for day care to be arranged outside the hospital (see p. 84). Day hospital care is similar to the programme of activities offered to inpatients which is described below, and may be offered on a weekly or daily basis. It may be an alternative to coming into hospital as an inpatient, or a way of easing the transition from hospital for people being discharged from inpatient care.

INPATIENT CARE

Procedures throughout the UK are broadly similar, although inevitably some hospitals have progressed faster than others in putting new ideas and philosophies into practice. This section aims to give you a realistic picture of what you can expect as a patient or relative. Chapter 11 gives details of your rights, and tells you how to make a complaint if you are dissatisfied by your experience. Complaining may be a positive step which not only helps yourself but also leads to changes and improvements which benefit others.

Admission to hospital

Sometimes admission to a mental health hospital is necessary so that treatment can be given with close support and supervision from hospital staff. The decision to offer hospital admission is taken by a psychiatrist and only after careful consideration of the circumstances, given that most people prefer care in their own homes, and that inpatient care is expensive for the health authority. The vast majority of people in mental health hospitals are 'informal' or voluntary patients. Occasionally people are detained for assessment or treatment under the Mental Health Act; the restrictions and rights which apply under the Act are covered in detail in Chapters 7 and 11.

When you are admitted to hospital you will be welcomed on to the ward by nursing staff, and soon after arrival you will be seen by a doctor. You will be given an opportunity to meet other patients and the professionals who will be involved in your care. Within the first 24 hours you should be introduced to the doctor who will work most closely with you, and you should be allocated a primary nurse. This nurse is responsible for your nursing care; he or she is the member of staff with whom you have most day-to-day contact, and with whom you can raise any problems or queries. You should also be offered written information about the unit or ward, the services available, and the hospital routine.

Bring with you your own day and night clothes, which you will wear while in hospital, toiletries, and enough money to buy items for day-to-day needs. Security for personal belongings can be a problem in some hospitals, so if possible avoid bringing anything valuable.

The treatment plan

All hospital patients are given their own treatment plan, which will be discussed with you by the doctor, nurse and other staff involved in your care. The plan is likely to include medication and a range of therapeutic groups and activities designed to help with any particular problems. Your medication will be regularly reviewed, with the aim of balancing effectiveness and side-effects, and this should be carefully explained by the doctor.

In most hospitals the treatment plan is reviewed at a weekly meeting of the hospital staff, often known as the ward round. Patients are usually invited to take part in these meetings and to be fully involved in discussion about their treatment. It can be quite intimidating to talk in front of a large number of professionals, but don't let yourself be put off. It is very important that you understand the recommended treatment and that the professionals take your views and experience into account. If you have relatives or a partner, they may occasionally be invited to these meetings, although if you prefer them not to attend you have a right to request the hospital staff not to ask them.

The hospital routine

The routine varies from hospital to hospital, and the activities you will take part in will depend on your particular needs and wishes. The daily programme is likely to include various therapeutic groups, relaxation classes, anxiety management and assertion training, as well as activities such as cookery, art, pottery, and music. When you are not involved in organised activities there are usually a variety of recreational facilities including television, newspapers, a library, music, board games, table tennis and snooker. Outings may be arranged to leisure facilities elsewhere. A typical day in hospital may look something like this:

7.30–8.00am	Get up, have medication
8.30–9.00am	Breakfast
9.30–10.30am	Therapeutic group on the ward
10.30–11.00am	Mid-morning tea or coffee
11.00–11.30am	Discussion of treatment with doctors and nurses in the ward round
12.30–1.30pm	Lunch (chosen from menu the day before)
2.00–3.30pm	Therapeutic activities, e.g. attending occupational therapy department for art therapy
3.30–6.00pm	Tea, leisure time
6.00–7.00pm	Supper
7.00–9.00pm	Leisure time, visitors
10.00–10.30pm	Hot drink, medication, go to bed

Visitors

Visiting hours are usually from late afternoon to about 9pm on weekdays, with open hours at weekends and public holidays. In some hospitals there are no restrictions as long as visits do not coincide with therapeutic activities. It is usually best to check with the nursing staff beforehand.

Home leave

The aim of hospital care is to help people recover and resume their normal life as soon as possible. Home leave for a day, a weekend or longer is often part of the treatment plan, and may be a helpful way of preparing for the transition from hospital. It should always be pre-planned so that proper arrangements can be made and the family are fully prepared. In some areas, particularly the inner cities, there is such pressure to admit new patients that existing ones are encouraged to have home leave without proper notice or planning. If you feel this is happening, and you are unhappy about it, bring the situation to the notice of your consultant psychiatrist or the hospital managers. (See Chapter 11 for details about your rights as a patient.)

If you are a detained patient under the Mental Health Act you may still be able to have home leave by agreement with the psychiatrist. Section 17 of the Act contains the relevant regulations. It is quite common for detained patients to be given extended home leave after a period of inpatient treatment. This may be for the remaining time the patient is liable to be detained, up to a maximum of six months, and the psychiatrist may attach certain conditions – for example living in a particular place and returning for outpatient appointments. The psychiatrist may recall you to hospital during this time. If you are absent without agreement, arrangements may be made for you to be returned to hospital.

Seclusion

Most psychiatric units or wards are not locked, although they may have a seclusion room which is used for patients who are acutely disturbed or having a violent episode. Seclusion rooms should never be used for punishment but only to hold patients for a brief period while they calm down, and for no longer than is absolutely necessary. Staff have a duty to record the use of seclusion, and these records are inspected by the Mental Health Act Commissioners on their periodic visits.

Leaving hospital

Most people remain in hospital for up to four weeks, although the length of stay depends on individual needs; some people are there for considerably longer. Leaving hospital is not usually the end of the treatment plan, but a continuing part of it, and arrangements are likely to be made which offer follow-up care and treatment through outpatient appointments or day care, or through support from the GP, a community mental health nurse or a social worker. Hospitals are required by Department of Health guidelines to prepare a care plan for every discharged patient. See Chapter 5 for details of these procedures, such as the care programme approach, Section 117 of the Mental Health Act, and needs assessments.

As with home leave, it is important that your discharge from hospital should be properly planned in advance. If you know of any problems at home which may make this difficult, inform the staff. When you are discharged you will usually be given a prescription for up to two weeks' supply of medication, together with a medical certificate for claiming benefit if necessary. Further prescriptions or certificates are then usually obtained either from your GP, or else from the outpatient department if this has been arranged. The hospital will send a letter to your GP informing him or her of your discharge from hospital and of the arrangements that have been set up for your future care and support.

Making your voice heard in hospital

Doctors, nurses and other hospital staff do their best to help meet the needs of inpatients. At the same time many hospitals recognise that patients may feel powerless and find it difficult to voice their concerns. It is an important part of treatment for patients to take control of their lives and to be able to express their views, and there are various ways in which more enlightened hospitals try to overcome this problem. Some invite **outside advocates from voluntary organisations** such as MIND to come and offer confidential advice and support to patients. Another idea is the **patients' council**, in which patients form a committee that does not include hospital staff. The members discuss issues of common concern, and where necessary take these up with hospital staff or management. Finally, **social workers** often work within hospitals and have a degree of independence since they are employed by the local authority. It may be helpful to approach a social worker for initial advice if you find it difficult to raise an issue through other channels.

SECURE HOSPITAL CARE

Locked wards

In keeping with the philosophy of greater freedom and of patients being treated in the least restrictive way, most psychiatric wards are not locked. Practice varies, however, and in some hospitals 'open' wards are locked at times to prevent a patient who is detained under the Mental Health Act from leaving. If this happens, the staff have a duty to make sure that all 'informal' patients are able to leave the ward as and when they choose.

Sometimes it is felt necessary for a patient to be cared for on a ward which is kept permanently locked. Some hospitals have a locked ward available, but if not the patient may have to be transferred to a locked ward in a hospital some distance away.

Regional secure units

People with a mental disorder who are caught up in the criminal justice system may be admitted to a regional secure unit in one of the following ways:

● they may be admitted straight from court under an order of the Mental Health Act.

● they may be transferred, under the Mental Health Act, from an ordinary psychiatric hospital because they need care in a more secure setting

● they may be transferred from prison under an order of the Mental Health Act

● they may be transferred from one of the special hospitals because they no longer need to be in conditions of maximum security

There are currently some 600 beds in regional secure units, with more planned, although the 1975 Butler Report recommended that 2,000 were needed and there is likely to be a shortfall for years to come. This means that some patients who need this level of security are being cared for in less secure settings, while others who no longer need maximum security are having to remain in special hospitals for longer than necessary. The regional secure units each serve a local area and generally provide more intensive care, with higher staff ratios than in ordinary hospitals.

Special hospitals

These hospitals provide conditions of maximum security for people who are mentally disordered and need this level of care and control. There are three special hospitals in England and one in Scotland:

Rampton Hospital
Retford
Notts DN22 0PD
Tel: 01777 248321

Ashworth Hospital
Maghull
Merseyside L31 1HL
Tel: 0151 473 0303

Broadmoor Hospital
Crowthorne
Berkshire RG11 7SG
Tel: 01344 773111

The State Hospital
Carstairs Junction
Lanark ML11 8RP
Tel: 01555 840293

Visiting can be difficult for relatives who live some distance away, although there is some special transport laid on from the larger cities. Concern has been expressed that the emphasis in special hospitals is focused too heavily on custody and not enough on care and treatment.

PRIVATE HOSPITALS

The number of private hospitals providing care and treatment for people with mental illness has grown in recent years. Their main advantage is that the physical environment offered is often much more attractive and comfortable than in NHS hospitals, with private rooms, en suite facilities and televisions. There is also likely to be a wider choice of menu. Fees vary but may be in the region of £175 to £300 per day for a room, with treatments and appointments with professional staff often costing extra. BUPA, PPP and many other insurers will fund private hospital care within the terms of the individual subscriber's agreement. But psychiatric treatment can be lengthy and your cover may be limited, so always check with the insurers before admission.

NHS hospitals in the inner cities often have serious bed shortages, and in these areas it is now increasingly common for NHS patients to be placed for this reason in private hospitals, paid for by the health authority. Because this is expensive, it is usually just a temporary arrangement and people are transferred to the local NHS hospital as soon as a bed becomes available.

There is no evidence that doctors and nurses in private hospitals have greater skill or commitment than their NHS counterparts, and the standards of treatment and care overall are probably equivalent. Private hospitals do not always have good links with other local resources, which can cause problems when leaving hospital. There are, however, a number of private hospitals which provide specialist care and these services are sometimes purchased by health authorities for NHS patients whose needs cannot be met within local NHS hospitals. These private establishments include **St Andrew's Hospital** and the hospitals run by **Partnerships in Care Ltd:**

St Andrew's Hospital
Billing Road
Northampton NN1 5DG
Tel: 01604 29696

Partnerships in Care Ltd
Kneesworth House
Bassingbourn-cum-
Kneesworth
Royston
Herts SG8 5JP
Tel: 01763 248912

7

Help in a Crisis

What is a crisis? • **Who to contact in a crisis** • **Mental health assessments and the Mental Health Act** • **Mental health and the criminal courts**

WHAT IS A CRISIS?

A crisis is a point at which a situation must change, and where some action or decision needs to be taken. A mental health crisis can arise in a number of different ways:

● mental illness sometimes involves a long, slow process of deterioration in a person's ability to lead a normal life; this may affect their relationships, their employment and housing situation as well as their emotional well-being, and eventually a crisis point may be reached

● the long-term effects of mental illness may make the person concerned less able or inclined to take action to seek help; stress may then build up to the point where family members or friends feel they can no longer cope and that something must be done

● a person who suffers from a serious mental illness may behave in ways which are unsafe or damaging for themselves or those around them, in which case urgent help is likely to be needed

● a major life event such as a bereavement, break-up of a relationship or loss of a job, or a combination of stressful events, may lead to a person's normal ability to cope breaking down; this can affect their mental health and a crisis point may be reached

For problems which are emotionally based or related to stress, crisis can be an important moment. At this time people's normal defences may be lowered, and they may open up and express themselves more easily or honestly. If skilled help is available quickly, positive changes can sometimes be made.

WHO TO CONTACT IN A CRISIS

The right person to contact depends on the situation and the kind of help needed, which may include:

- talking to someone for support and advice
- arranging for medical treatment
- help in preventing harm or violence

If there is already a professional worker involved, such as a doctor, social worker or community psychiatric nurse, it is usually best to contact that person first. If not, there are a number of options which are described below.

It is a particular irony that crises often happen outside the working hours of professionals. Problems which seem manageable during the day or during the week can build up to crisis point in the evening or at the weekend. The lack of support available at these times may increase your anxiety and can in itself contribute to a crisis developing. Fortunately this problem is becoming more widely recognised, and out-of-hours services are slowly being developed.

Special crisis services

CRISIS INTERVENTION TEAMS

In a few areas local mental health professionals operate a crisis intervention service where a team of professionals, usually a doctor and a social worker or nurse, make quick contact with people in crisis and their families. They assess what is going on and if necessary provide intensive support for a brief period, to enable people to regain control over their lives and, if possible, avoid admission to hospital.

CRISIS ADVICE SERVICES
There are also a small but growing number of local crisis services offering advice and help to people through a telephone helpline or a walk-in advice service. Many of these are run by professionals based in community mental health centres or hospitals, although these are seldom open 24 hours.

CRISIS HOUSES
An idea popular with users, which is more developed in the United States than in this country, is the crisis house or safe house. It provides a safe haven in a non-medical setting for people going through a crisis. The women's refuge movement has demonstrated the success of this approach in supporting women faced with domestic violence. However, professionals in Britain are generally cautious of offering residential crisis support to people with serious mental health problems without first giving them a thorough assessment, and unless there are enough staff to provide the intensive support which may be needed.

Professional help available

The special services described above are not available in many areas, and it is therefore very important to be aware of the other options and to make the right choice. Help in a crisis can be available from a number of sources, particularly from the following:

GENERAL PRACTITIONERS
GPs can advise about medical treatment and about dealing with stress. In an emergency, contact your GP and either arrange for an urgent appointment at the surgery or ask for a home visit if one is needed. GPs' surgeries should provide

24-hour cover, although outside normal hours it is often provided by doctors from a deputising service who will not be familiar with the person concerned. The doctor will assess the situation and may prescribe medication or arrange an appointment for the person to see a psychiatrist, or for some other help. The GP is responsible for arranging hospital admission where necessary. (See Chapter 4 for more details about the work of GPs in mental health.)

SOCIAL WORKERS

Specialist mental health social workers can offer advice and support about problems in coping with mental illness. They may be able to arrange for help through a respite stay in a residential care hostel or at a day centre. Specially trained approved social workers also have a particular responsibility to assess the needs of a person in a mental health crisis. This is explained in detail on p. 113–17. Social work offices usually have a duty system for responding to urgent requests for help, and have arrangements to cover emergencies out of office hours. (See p. 60 for further details of mental health social workers and how to contact them.)

COMMUNITY PSYCHIATRIC NURSES

CPNs give medication in the home and offer support through home visits. In some areas they also provide an emergency service. If a CPN is not involved already, you usually have to ask for this service through your GP. (see p. 58 for more about CPNs.)

HOSPITAL

Admission to hospital may sometimes be necessary, and can be arranged through a GP as described above. A small number of hospitals run emergency psychiatric clinics where people can be seen by a doctor without appointment. If medical help is needed urgently and for some reason it cannot be arranged through your GP, go to the local hospital casualty or accident and emergency department and ask to be seen by a doctor; if there is a psychiatric department at the hospital a duty doctor with experience of psychiatry may be available. It is also worth bearing in mind that there are trained psychiatric nurses on duty on inpatient psychiatric hospital wards in the evenings and at weekends when other professionals can be very thin on the ground. Hospital nurses are usually fully occupied caring for patients but a phone call to the staff in the psychiatric ward may be helpful if you really cannot obtain advice from the GP or social services.

POLICE

In an emergency phone 999. The police can be called if there is immediate risk to life and limb. It is possible that this could result in a person being charged with a criminal offence, although if the offence is not a serious one and the person is mentally unwell, this should not happen.

Occasionally a mental health professional responding to an emergency may ask the police to be present as a precaution, to make sure that everyone is safe. Under Section 136 of the Mental Health Act the police also have powers to remove a mentally disordered person from any public place to 'a place of safety' for up to 72 hours. This should be followed by a mental health assessment as soon as possible. The place of safety is usually the local hospital, although it can be a police cell. (See below for more details about the Mental Health Act and mental health assessments.)

Other help in a crisis

If you experience difficulty getting help from the professionals mentioned above, contact one of the following organisations which may be able to give advice:

SANELINE

Tel: 01345 678000 (calls charged at local rate); tel: 0171 724 8000 (if calling from London) helpline every day of the year 2pm–midnight.

A national telephone helpline for people with mental health problems and their carers. Saneline staff, who are

111

trained volunteers, have access to information about resources throughout the UK. They can help people get in touch with local agencies as well as supply general information and provide support.

MIND

Tel: 0181 519 2122; Scottish Association for Mental Health tel: 0131 229 9687; Northern Ireland Association for Mental Health tel: 01232 328474

The leading mental health voluntary organisation, it has a large number of local branches throughout England and Wales, with similar associations in Scotland and Northern Ireland. The local branches may be able to give you advice and assistance about getting help in a crisis, and will be familiar with local resources. Telephone numbers of local branches can be obtained from Saneline or from the national head office. (For more details of MIND regional offices and addresses, see pp. 91–3).

THE NATIONAL SCHIZOPHRENIA FELLOWSHIP (NSF)

Telephone numbers of local branches can be obtained from Saneline above, or from the national head offices: NSF (England and Wales) Tel: 0181 547 3937; NSF (Scotland) Tel: 0131 226 2025; NSF (Northern Ireland) Tel: 01232 248006

A voluntary organisation with local branches in many areas. Local NSF offices may be able to help with advice and information about dealing with a crisis involving any serious mental illness (not just schizophrenia), and can be particularly supportive to carers or relatives. (For more details of NSF regional offices and addresses see pp. 141–2.)

SAMARITANS

Tel: 01753 532713 (head office). Ring this number for details of local 24-hour confidential telephone advice service.

Telephone numbers of local branches can also be obtained from your local phone book or from Saneline.

MENTAL HEALTH ASSESSMENTS AND THE MENTAL HEALTH ACT

This section explains the basis of hospital admission and guardianship under the Mental Health Act. The legal language used is not user-friendly, although in the interests of accuracy and clarity we have kept as closely as possible to the terms used in the Act. Rights and safeguards under the Act are covered in Chapter 11. Further information about restrictions on patients is given in Chapters 3, 5 and 6.

The Mental Health Act 1983 is the relevant Act of Parliament in England and Wales which lays down how people with a mental disorder may be admitted to hospital. It includes voluntary admissions and those occasions where admission takes place against a person's wishes, which is often known as being 'sectioned'. Compulsory admission and detention in hospital is very much a last resort, arranged only if the grounds set out in the relevant section of the Mental Health Act are met and if there is no suitable alternative. The starting point is a formal mental health assessment.

Mental health assessments

A formal mental health assessment under the Mental Health Act is different from other kinds of assessment, as it focuses on whether there are grounds for the person to be admitted to hospital under the terms of the Act. It normally requires three people:

- a doctor (usually the GP) who knows the person being assessed

- an approved doctor who has particular experience in the diagnosis and treatment of mental illness

- an approved social worker (ASW) who has had special training in mental health assessment

Anyone can ask for a mental health assessment with a view to hospital admission to be considered, although the law gives special status to a person's nearest relative (see p. 135 for a definition of this term). If the nearest relative asks for an assessment, the ASW must take the case into consideration and give reasons in writing if a compulsory admission does not result. The nearest relative may also make an application for compulsory admission, but the code of practice that accompanies the Act advises that the ASW should usually be the applicant and that in all cases an ASW must be involved in the assessment. The responsibility for arranging an assessment rests with the ASW, who also makes the practical arrangements for taking the person into hospital if that is the outcome. The ASW has a duty to consider all the circumstances; he or she will try to obtain as much information as possible and will usually have a number of discussions with family members and professionals before going ahead with a formal assessment.

The assessment team will want to arrange for any treatment to be carried out in the least restrictive conditions possible, although they do have the legal authority to admit a person to hospital under a Section of the Mental Health Act if it is necessary for the health or safety of the person or for the protection of others.

The admission Sections of the Mental Health Act

- **Section 2 admission for assessment** for up to 28 days in the interests of the patient's health or safety or with a view to the protection of others. The person must be suffering from a mental disorder of a nature or degree which warrants detention for assessment. The ASW or nearest relative may make the application, founded on two doctors' recommendations.
Treatment may be given, as with a Section 3, and in some circumstances this may be without the consent of the patient.

- **Section 3 admission for treatment** for up to six months in the interests of the patient's health or safety or for the protection of others.

Section 3 is likely to be used when the hospital knows the person being assessed and is clear about the treatment needed. Section 3 needs the consent of the nearest relative (see Chapter 11). The person must be suffering from one of the following mental disorders of a nature or degree where hospital treatment is appropriate:

– mental illness
– severe mental impairment
– mental impairment ⎱ where treatment is likely to
– psychopathic disorder ⎰ alleviate or prevent deterioration

An application is made as under Section 2.

• **Section 4 emergency admission for assessment** for up to 72 hours where admission is urgently needed and a Section 2 assessment would involve undesirable delay. An application is made by an ASW or nearest relative, founded on one doctor's recommendation. There is no power to treat the person against their wishes.

• **Section 5 (2) detention of informal patients** for up to 72 hours on the recommendation of the hospital doctor in charge of treatment. This applies to people who have been informally admitted to hospital. There is no power to treat the person against their wishes, and a proper mental health assessment should be arranged as soon as possible. Under Section 5 (4) a nurse may authorise detention for up to six hours if a doctor is not available.

• **Section 136 police power to remove to a place of safety** for up to 72 hours. This applies to a person who is in a public place and who appears to be mentally disordered and in immediate need of care or control. The place of safety is likely to be a hospital. There is no power to treat the person against their wishes, and an ASW and a doctor must be involved in a further assessment as soon as possible.

115

- **Section 135 court warrant:** an ASW can apply to a magistrate for a warrant authorising the police, accompanied by an ASW and a doctor, to gain entry and, if thought fit, to remove a person to a place of safety for up to 72 hours. There must be reasonable grounds to suspect that the person is suffering from a mental disorder and is being neglected, ill-treated or not under proper control; or, if living alone, that the person is unable to care for themselves. The effect is exactly the same as with Section 136.

What happens when someone is sectioned?

Once the two doctors and the approved social worker or nearest relative have decided to use one of the above sections, they must sign the legal forms and should explain to the person what this means. The ASW will then arrange for the person to be taken to hospital, usually in an ambulance. On arrival, the detained person should be given a leaflet explaining their rights, including their right to appeal against detention. The ASW must also tell the nearest relative of their rights. Because this involves removing choice, liberty and personal responsibility from an individual, it is vital that people know their rights; those of both patients and nearest relatives are explained in detail in Chapter 11.

Guardianship

A mental health assessment may also result in an application for guardianship under Section 7. This does not involve admission to hospital, but has the effect of placing a person under the guardianship of either the local authority or someone approved by them. The guardian may require the person to live in a particular place; to attend for treatment, occupation, education or training; and to give access to any doctor, ASW or specified person. As with Section 3, guardianship lasts for six months initially, and the nearest relative must agree to the application. Although the person can be 'required to attend for treatment', there is no authority to *give* treatment without consent. Guardianship was not very widely used in the past, but as a result of current concerns about care in the community various organisations have pressed for it to be considered more often, and there are signs of a significant increase in its use.

Scotland

The Mental Health (Scotland) Act 1984 allows for **application for admission**, similar to a Section 3, for up to six months; the application must be submitted to the Sheriff, with the patient and nearest relative having the opportunity of raising objections. The only other admission section is for **emergency admission**, which is similar to a Section 4 but may be extended to **short-term detention** for up to 28 days on the recommendation of one doctor; unlike the situation in England, Wales and Northern Ireland, it is possible for admission to be arranged on one doctor's authority alone, although the doctor must try to obtain the consent of the nearest relative or a mental health officer. The mental health officer is the Scottish equivalent of the approved social worker, and plays a similar role. The Mental Welfare Commission must be informed of all detentions, and has the power to discharge patients.

Northern Ireland

The Mental Health (Northern Ireland) Order 1986 provides for **admission for assessment** on application by an approved social worker or nearest relative, based on one medical recommendation, usually that of the GP. The person must be seen by a consultant psychiatrist within 48 hours. Admission is initially for 14 days for assessment, but can be extended for treatment for up to six months on the basis of two further medical recommendations. Unlike the provisions of English, Welsh and Scottish law, psychopathic disorder is excluded as a category for compulsory admission. Another difference is that doctors' holding powers, and police pow-

117

ers to remove a person from a public place to a place of safety, are limited to 48 hours.

MENTAL HEALTH AND THE CRIMINAL COURTS

Many people with a mental disorder come before the courts, usually as a result of minor offences. In various parts of the country court schemes have been set up to provide on-the-spot assessment and advice by mental health professionals, so as to prevent people being sentenced for offences when they really need help or treatment. Another option open to the courts, if hospital treatment is not needed, is to make a probation order with a requirement that the person receives outpatient psychiatric treatment.

Under Part 3 of the Mental Health Act, magistrates' courts and higher courts can order mentally disordered offenders to be detained in hospital on the basis of medical advice. An order may be made for observation and reports, or under **Section 37** the court may order detention in hospital for treatment, with the same effect as a Section 3; restrictions may be added under some circumstances which prevent the person's discharge without the Home Secretary's permission (Section 41). The court can also make a guardianship order, with the same effect as Section 7.

8

Suicide, Self-harm and Violence

The incidence of suicide • Causes of suicide • Suicide and mental illness • Suicide risk • Attempted suicide and parasuicide • Deliberate self-harm • Causes of violence • Violence and mental illness

---

Suicide, self-harm and violence are uncomfortable subjects to read about or even think about. They are a part of human experience which causes fear and distress and which many of us would, quite reasonably, rather avoid. If, however, you have concerns about your own behaviour, or that of a friend or relative, it may be helpful to know the risks involved, how seriously to take them and what can be done to help.

THE INCIDENCE OF SUICIDE

Not until 1961 did suicide or attempted suicide cease to be treated as a crime in the UK, reflecting a long cultural and religious tradition in which the act of a person taking their own life has been seen as going against the laws of nature. The relationship between suicide and mental illness is complex – clearly not all suicides are the result of 'mental illness', although it can be a factor; emotional distress or disturbance must be involved to some degree for both the person concerned and those around them.

119

Government statistics show that the overall suicide rate in the UK is 11.1 per 100,000 population, and that there are over 4000 suicides each year. This is roughly the same as the number of deaths from road traffic accidents. The suicide rate is significantly higher for some groups of people. Doctors, for example, have a much higher rate than the rest of the population, which perhaps mirrors both the high stress levels of their work and their specialist knowledge and access to medicines.

The incidence of suicide in people with a serious mental illness is considerably higher than the norm, at around 15 per cent. In the *Health of the Nation* White Paper, published in 1992, the government announced its aim that by the year 2000 the suicide rate for mentally ill people should be reduced by at least a third, to no more than 10 per cent.

CAUSES OF SUICIDE

The difference between suicide rates for different groups of people indicates a complex set of individual and social factors. When someone takes their own life there are personal causes and a meaning behind their action – it may, for example, be a reaction to a distressing life event or severe disappointment, an expression of hopelessness about the future, a gesture of anger, or an escape from intolerable pressures. Psychoanalytic theory views suicide as a form of displacement, in which angry and murderous feelings towards others are turned inwards.

Sociological research into suicide statistics suggests links with wider social factors. Suicide may, for instance, result from an individual's lack of integration within society or within the family – suicide rates are higher in societies where community and family ties are relatively weak. Unemployment and changing patterns of marriage and divorce may also have an impact on suicide rates. If an individual whose life has been regulated by the social conventions of work or marriage is faced with a major upset such as redundancy or divorce they may be unable to cope with the emotional and practical consequences. At that point they may be at greater risk of committing suicide.

SUICIDE AND MENTAL ILLNESS

The higher-than-average suicide rate among people with mental illness applies particularly to those suffering from severe depression, manic-depressive illness or schizophrenia. In some cases suicidal thoughts may be related to delusional ideas and are therefore linked to psychosis. Even with a person who has a diagnosis of schizophrenia, however, the predominant factor in taking their own life may be a sense of depression and hopelessness about the future. The risk of suicide has been found to be high amongst people discharged after a period of treatment in a psychiatric hospital, especially in the first month after leaving.

People who are severely depressed sometimes have thoughts of ending their lives. Paradoxically, the risk of active suicidal behaviour is less in the most severe depression. This is because in extreme cases the person is so lacking in drive and motivation that they do not have the capacity to act on their suicidal thoughts. The risk is therefore highest where the person has expressed suicidal ideas, and is depressed, but still has enough insight and energy to take action. This means that people undergoing treatment for depression may need as much care and support when their mental state is starting to improve as they do when they are in decline.

Social isolation and lack of support are obvious dangers with mental illness. There is some concern that the programme of closure for the large old psychiatric hospitals, combined with the inadequacy of care in the community, has led to an increase in the suicide rate for people with a mental illness.

SUICIDE RISK

Research into suicide rates reveals a number of factors which point to some people being more likely than others to commit suicide (although suicide is still uncommon, even among these groups of people).

Increased-risk groups

- people with a psychotic illness, especially schizophrenia
- people who are severely depressed
- people with a history of persistent alcohol or drug misuse
- people who are bereaved, particularly if they have lost their spouse
- men have a three times higher suicide rate than women; men over the age of 50 and young men of 15–24 are particularly at risk
- younger Asian women
- people who are unemployed, or have lost their job
- people with a physical illness
- people who are either single or divorced are at higher risk than married people
- people who live alone
- childless people

ATTEMPTED SUICIDE AND PARASUICIDE

'Parasuicide' is a term sometimes used by mental health professionals to describe the behaviour of people who make suicidal gestures but do not in fact intend to end their lives. It is very difficult to be certain what a person's intentions are, and whether their actions represent a genuine suicide attempt or a cry for help. Usually not even they themselves are fully aware of their motives and intentions. With some people suicidal behaviour appears to be a gamble with death. Attempts to gain attention through suicidal gestures also tend to be inherently dangerous and carry with them the risk of things going wrong.

For every successful suicide it has been estimated that there are approximately 30 failed attempts. The degree of seriousness of the attempt can be gauged to some extent according to the following factors.

Indicators of serious suicide attempt

- evidence of active, deliberate preparation, e.g. obtaining drugs
- other preparations, e.g. putting financial affairs in order, making a will
- planning to be alone, with no one else nearby
- timing the attempt so that others are unlikely to be able to intervene
- taking precautions against discovery, e.g. locking the door
- not acting to get help after the attempt
- telling someone of the suicidal intention beforehand
- writing a suicide note
- previous history of suicide attempts

The incidence of parasuicide is highest among women during their late teens and early twenties. It is often an unplanned, impulsive act in response to domestic conflict or a stressful life event.

What can be done to help?

Suicidal thoughts are not uncommon –they can be taken as a warning sign that things are going wrong and that something should be done to review the situation. Both the person concerned and others who may be affected are likely to be in need of professional support. Here are some suggestions:

- getting help and support from a trusted person can be of benefit; talking about feelings and the reasons for them can help to give some understanding of what is going on, and suggest changes which may need to be made or that it is time to seek professional help

- if support from friends and family is not available, or not helpful, personal counselling may help; see Chapter 5 for details of counselling services. The Samaritans (see p. 112) are always available on the end of the telephone

- the GP is a good starting point for professional help; depression may be at the root of the problem and the doctor may be able to prescribe medication or arrange for other help, e.g. specialist counselling or psychotherapy

- if there is a treatable mental illness involved, its treatment should be a priority

- it may be helpful to make a record of thoughts and events, to keep track of danger signs

- situations which lead to suicidal thoughts should be avoided if possible, or else ways of dealing with them should be explored with the help of a skilled mental health professional

- it may be helpful to rehearse strategies for acting and seeking help when suicidal thoughts occur

One of the issues to be faced with suicidal behaviour is the strong feelings that it arouses. A person who has made an attempt at suicide may feel despair and anger at having been prevented from carrying out their wishes. People close to them may be angry, guilty or ashamed about what has happened. Professionals, too, are not immune to feelings and sometimes show an unsympathetic attitude, which is not likely to help.

In practice, many people who attempt suicide end up in the accident and emergency department of their local hospital. Most hospitals arrange for a doctor with psychiatric experience to see people thought to be suicidal, so that further help or treatment can be provided if needed. Sometimes the risk of suicide is so great that hospital admission for psychiatric treatment is set up. If there is evidence of a mental disorder, compulsory action under the Mental Health

Act may be considered. Hospitals have protocols for close observation of people who are felt to be actively suicidal, so that they are not left on their own.

If a person commits suicide, their partner, family and close friends are likely to suffer particular distress and to need support and counselling. See Chapter 5 for details of counselling and other help available.

DELIBERATE SELF-HARM

Some people harm themselves deliberately in a way which is not life-threatening, and which cannot be considered suicidal as there is clearly no intention to cause death. The range of self-harming behaviour is wide, although it most commonly involves cutting or burning the skin or swallowing harmful liquids and objects. It is occasionally, although not usually, related to a mental illness.

Skin-cutting is perhaps the most frequent form of deliberate self-harm, and is most common amongst women in their teens and early twenties. In our society is is regarded as abnormal and disturbed behaviour. People who harm themselves in this way probably do so either as a means of relieving stress or as a way of achieving excitement. It is said to dull feelings of emotional pain more than to cause pain, and may be an expression of psychological scars resulting from abuse in childhood.

What can be done to help?

Although it is difficult to understand, and there are differing views and theories, persistent deliberate self-harm is likely to be related either to some deep unhappiness and emotional disturbance, or occasionally to a psychotic illness. If it is the latter, psychiatric care and treatment will be needed. Where the problems are emotionally based the person will be in need of support, and counselling or psychotherapy may be helpful. In either case a referral to a psychiatrist is probably advisable for a specialist assessment of the nature of the problem, and to work out the best treatment.

CAUSES OF VIOLENCE

It is a common misconception that there is a link between mental illness and violence, but this is not generally true. Violence can result from a variety of causes – in fact it is a common response which may be seen as either acceptable (such as a boxing match) or unacceptable, according to the situation. In most domestic situations violence is unacceptable and indicates the existence of a serious problem.

Violent behaviour clearly involves a number of social factors, for example the way in which boys in particular are brought up to relate to society, and the role models for violence which can be seen throughout the media. Links also exist between the rate of violent crime and levels of unemployment.

At an individual level, violence can be seen in a number of ways:

- it may be a reaction to general stress or frustration, i.e. taking it out on someone else

- it may occur within a relationship as an expression of extreme anger towards the victim

- it may be behaviour which has been learnt as a 'normal' part of everyday life

- less commonly, the person who is being violent may behave in this way because they enjoy exercising power or inflicting pain

- violence is often associated with alcohol misuse

VIOLENCE AND MENTAL ILLNESS

Although people with a mental illness are no more likely to

be violent than others, when they do threaten violence it can be serious. A number of well-publicised tragedies testify to this. Mental illness can lead to high levels of stress and frustration for the sufferer, which can sometimes cause a violent outburst. Stressful family relationships can be at the root of such violence, and it is often those closest to the person who become the victims.

Occasionally mental illness is more directly the cause of violence. Violence is sometimes related to depression, manic depression or schizophrenia. People suffering from schizophrenia are not on the whole likely to be violent, despite the widely held belief to the contrary. When violence does occur it may be linked to a delusion which others may be unaware of, and is therefore difficult to predict. The victim may be perceived as some kind of threat or danger – for example part of a conspiracy, or looking at the person in a critical way. In manic-depressive illness, when a person is in the manic phase they may feel enormously frustrated and angered by the actions of others who are felt to be getting in the way. Objects may then be thrown, or the person may suddenly hit out. Some people suffering from dementia become cantankerous and also hit out, either from sheer frustration or from the effects of the dementia on their emotional state.

In these situations, anyone else involved must take precautions for their personal safety. Situations can often be defused by adopting a calm, non-confrontational approach and making it clear to the potentially violent person that you do not pose a threat.

What can be done to help?

The first requirement for people who behave in a violent way as a direct or indirect result of mental illness is care and treatment for that illness.

The majority of people who become violent are not mentally ill, but may still need help. Counselling may enable a person to understand their behaviour and its effect on others, and to find alternative ways of dealing with their emotions. A few counsellors offer individual or group therapy for people who have problems coping with their own aggression. It is also possible to ask a GP for a referral to a psychiatrist or psychologist, who may be able to help by assessing the problem and arranging treatment if appropriate.

If a person behaves in a violent way, there will also be a victim who needs help. Victims may be traumatised by their experience and may need skilled counselling. In addition to the counselling resources listed in Chapter 5 the following may be helpful:

There is a national network of **Victim Support Schemes** where trained volunteers offer practical and emotional support. For details contact your local Citizens' Advice Bureau, police or the national association of victim support schemes:

***Victim Support* (Head Office)**
39 Brixton Road
London SW9 6DZ
Tel: 0171 735 9166

The **Criminal Injuries Compensation Board** can make payments to victims of violence. Contact your local Citizens' Advice Bureau or a solicitor, or else ask the Board to send you an application form:

Criminal Injuries Compensation Board
Whittington House
19 Alfred Place
London WC1E 7LG
Tel: 0171 335 6800

9

Help for Carers

WHO IS A CARER?

A carer is a relative or friend who provides care and support to another person by either sharing their home or contributing in some other way. Across the country there are thousands of carers for someone with a mental health problem. They are ordinary people with no special skills or training and come from all walks of life and many different cultural, religious and ethnic backgrounds. Their circumstances will vary enormously depending on their income, the severity of the mental health problem and the help and support available locally. Carers may be elderly and perhaps worried about future care, or may be young and totally bewildered by their parents' behaviour.

THE EXPERIENCE OF CARING

What does it feel like when, after years of happy marriage, your husband will not talk to you because the voices tell him you are an impostor? What does it feel like when the son you have loved and cherished and seen through his A-levels turns up on your doorstep, dirty and dishevelled, and threatens to slash his wrists in front of you? What does a ten-year-old child feel like when his mother will not let him go out to play with his friends because she believes an evil spirit will kill him if he leaves the house? These and similar situations may be part of your experience as a carer. In concentrating on the treatment and care of the person who is ill, you may find that both your own needs as a carer and the contribution you can make are in danger of being overlooked.

Caring for another person can be very difficult and demanding in any circumstances, but when the person has a mental illness additional pressures are often heaped up. There can be a distinctly detrimental effect on 'normal' relationships, and families have to face the additional burden of stigma. Life can sometimes appear like a long melodrama, with alternating periods of stability, crisis, respite and recovery. Caring can be rewarding, but it can also be accompanied by painful, intense feelings such as guilt, fear, embarrassment, shame, frustration and anger. Living with and caring for a person who is mentally ill can be exhausting accompanied by a sense of always being on duty. This can naturally lead to feelings of resentment. And carers sometimes experience a feeling of loss for the person they once knew before mental illness entered their lives.

CARING IN A CRISIS

A particularly difficult time for carers occurs when a relative or friend is going into crisis (see Chapter 7). It is often those closest to the person who are the first to see the signs of decline, and yet they are not always able to convince mental health professionals. There is a danger, however, that normal behaviour can be mislabelled as symptomatic of mental illness. For example, if someone wants to spend time on their own they may not necessarily be getting ill. Every individual is firstly a unique person and only secondly do they have symptoms of mental illness.

The decision to seek help in a crisis will often be very painful, attended by feelings of guilt at needing respite and a sense of failure or powerlessness at not being able to avert the situation. Situations leading to a crisis can include someone becoming withdrawn and unresponsive, not eating or caring for themselves, and, at the other extreme, being out of control and behaving in a bizarre and unacceptable way.

Although people who have a mental illness are no more violent than anyone else, when a crisis is looming those who are closest are often on the receiving end of unpredictable behaviour including threats and aggression. It is therefore helpful to work out beforehand what to do in the event of a violent situation. Try to talk the person round using a calm voice, but if you are unable to manage the situation yourself, you should seek help. If the situation remains unsafe, do consider your own safety and remove yourself from the scene. This may be a difficult decision, particularly if you are concerned that the person may harm him/herself, but there may be no alternative if you are unable to contain the situation or prevent serious harm. If you need to prevent someone who is potentially violent from entering your home enquire at a Citizens Advice Bureau or your local law centre about taking out an injunction in the courts. (Help in a crisis is more fully dealt with in Chapter 7.)

CARERS' NEEDS

Caring can be a source of great stress and can deeply affect the quality of life. There is no doubt that an improvement in the quantity, quality and range of mental health services would improve the carer's lot immeasurably. Meanwhile, if carers' needs as detailed below are met, they are much more likely to be able to continue their role and to perform it effectively.

The task of caring is both important and difficult – what carers need above all is **acknowledgement,** to make them feel valued. They also need comprehensive **information** about issues ranging from benefits and services to the particular mental illness that they are coping with and what treatments are available.

You may often feel drained by your caring role and may need opportunities for **respite** – taking a break for short spells or longer periods so that you can relax and have time to yourself, perhaps even go on holiday, while someone else is looking after your friend or relative. When you feel at breaking point you may also need some opportunity for relief. If not, you run the risk of becoming exhausted and short-tempered and suffering disturbed sleep. If you do get to this stage, you may be unable to continue caring. It is therefore important to tell the professionals involved in your relative's care that you need help.

Carers also need **support**. You may find this is in short supply from friends, family and neighbours who may react with embarrassment or fear and not want to know. Support from professionals or from self-help groups can therefore be of crucial importance. In many areas there are carer's support groups which try to create a relaxed and confidential environment in which to share your experiences and feelings with other carers. Attending these groups can also be a good way of finding out about resources, rights and ways to cope with stress and anxiety.

CARERS AS PARTNERS IN TREATMENT

As a carer you may be able to make an important contribution to the success of a care plan for the person recovering from mental illness. You should, therefore, be able to share your views with professionals, to be listened to, and to be involved in care planning (see Chapter 11 about carers' rights). Although this sounds like common sense, it has taken a long time for mental health professionals to recognise the potential value of families and relatives, to start to include them in discussions about care plans and to offer them active support and guidance.

132

Helpful and unhelpful emotional environments

A number of research studies have shown that people with a serious mental illness, such as schizophrenia or manic depression, do not respond well to social relationships where a lot of intense emotions are being expressed. This has important implications for carers. Living with a person who has a mental illness can be very stressful and can naturally lead to emotions being felt and expressed, often in a negative and critical way, which can make matters worse. This is not, however, a case for blame or guilt but rather a case for guiding, supporting and valuing carers in making their own vital contribution to the care and treatment of the person.

Liz Kuipers, consultant clinical psychologist at the Institute of Psychiatry, has developed some useful guidelines, based on research findings which give pointers to what is helpful and unhelpful in maintaining good mental health:

Helpful	Unhelpful
Undemanding emotionally	Demanding, critical
Calm	Pressurised
Tolerant	Intolerant, angry, intrusive
Realistic expectations	Unrealistic expectations
Encourage new skills and acknowledge small achievements	Ignore and devalue progress
Optimistic	Pessimistic

Overstimulation and understimulation are both unhelpful for a person with a serious mental illness. Emotional overstimulation can lead to a worsening of psychotic symptoms, increased anxiety and behaviour which may be socially or physically damaging. Understimulation can result in withdrawal or overdependent, childlike behaviour. Carers and professionals should aim for the middle path, achieving the right balance of emotional stimulation and positive encouragement while not becoming overinvolved or overcontrolling.

NEAREST RELATIVES UNDER THE MENTAL HEALTH ACT

The Mental Health Act 1983 gives a number of rights and responsibilities to what is called the nearest relative. This only applies where powers under the Act are being considered or used, and at other times the role has no significance.

Who is the nearest relative

The nearest relative cannot be chosen by the person concerned, or by a professional, in the same way as a next of kin. This means that they may not necessarily be the relative most closely involved or best equipped to carry out the role. The definition is precisely set out in Section 26 of the Mental Health Act. The nearest relative is the person who comes nearest the top of the following list, with precedence given to the older if there is more than one relative of the same description.

- husband or wife, (except where permanently separated or where one partner has deserted the other)
- partner of the opposite sex, where cohabiting for not less than six months
- son or daughter
- father or mother
- brother or sister
- grandparent
- grandchild
- uncle or aunt
- nephew or niece
- anyone who has lived together with the person for not less than five years, providing there is no other relative

The only exceptions to this list are:

- where a relative on the list lives with or cares for the person, they take precedence
- where a relative does not normally live in the UK they are disregarded
- no one under 18 years of age can be a nearest relative, unless they are the husband, wife, father or mother
- where a nearest relative has been displaced by the county court (see p. 181)

The role of the nearest relative

The nearest relative is given an important legal status and professionals must assist them, consult with them, give them information, and carry out their instructions under certain circumstances. The rights and powers of nearest relatives are described more fully in Chapter 11. There are also several very practical ways in which the nearest relative can help:

- they can help to ensure that the needs of their relative are properly explained to professionals, and their rights protected

- they can support their relative through the process of a mental health assessment, and possibly admission to hospital

- they can give the views and wishes of the family about what should happen, as well as helping professionals to understand the background to the situation

- they can speak out or complain if they are not happy about decisions made or care and treatment given by professionals

Sometimes the role and responsibilities of being a nearest relative may seem an unwelcome burden which might cause undue pressure and damage family relationships. It is entirely up to the nearest relative to decide how far they wish to be involved. If they prefer not to act as nearest relative, they are not compelled to take any action, but the Act allows them to nominate any other suitable person (not necessarily someone on the list) to take on the role. This requires the signed agreement of both parties; an ASW from the local social services can advise about this procedure.

WHERE TO GO FOR HELP

Depending on where you live, there should be a range of statutory services available to you. These may include group and one-to-one support, respite care, holiday schemes, and advice and information. An increasing amount of support is also available from the voluntary sector. The following is a list of resources for carers of people with mental health problems, including addiction and dependency:

National carers' resources

For details of other carers' projects not listed here contact the MIND regional office for your area, or Scottish or Irish Mental Health Association (see pp. 91–93).

Al-Anon Family Groups
61 Great Dover Street
London SE1 4YF
Tel: 0171 403 0888 (24-hour confidential helpline covering England, Scotland, Wales and Northern Ireland)

Provides help and support for relatives and friends of alcoholics. (Alateen, a part of Al-Anon, is for teenagers who are affected by the problem drinking of a relative or close friend.) There are over 1000 self-help groups throughout the UK and Eire. A range of books, leaflets and pamphlets is available.

Alzheimer's Disease Society
Gordon House
10 Greencoat Place

London SW10 1PH
Tel: 0171 306 0606

24-hour freephone lines with recorded information and advice on Alzheimer's disease and other dementias, including sources of practical, financial and legal help: 0800 318771 (Alzheimer's disease); 0800 318772 (other dementias); 0800 318773 (Alzheimer's Disease Society); 0800 318774 (Who Can Help? services); 0800 318775 (legal and financial information).

Supports families across England, Wales and Northern Ireland through a network of branches (which may run day centres or sitting services), support groups and contact people. All local organisers have experience either of looking after someone with dementia or of working with the problem.

The Society also produces a regular newsletter for members and a publications list which includes leaflets aimed at helping carers with the management of the disease.

The information contained on the recorded message telephone lines may also be obtained on an audio-cassette by sending £3 to the above address (free to people who are visually impaired).

Alzheimer's Scotland Action on Dementia
8 Hill Street
Edinburgh EH2 3JZ
Tel: 0131 225 1453 (24-hour dementia helpline 0131 220 6155)

Provides a network of local services across Scotland including day centres, carers' support groups, home care services, befriending, information and benefits advice.

Association of Crossroads Care Attendant Schemes
10 Regent Place
Rugby
Warwickshire CV21 2PN
Tel: 01788 573653

Crossroads is the major national organisation providing a respite service for carers. Their service is aimed at relieving the stresses experienced by carers and people with physical, mental or sensory impairment within the family home through the provision of community-based care attendants who enable carers to have a few hours' break. There are over 30 autonomous local schemes across England, Scotland, Wales and Northern Ireland who are affiliated to the national Association.

Carers' National Association
20–25 Glasshouse Yard
London EC1A 4JS
Tel: 0171 490 8818 (general office). Carers' helpline 0171 490 8898 (Monday – Friday 1–4pm offers advice, support and details of local carers' support groups. Carers calling from a distance are welcome to leave their number and their call will be returned.)

For all carers, whether the people being cared for are physically or mentally ill, disabled or elderly and frail. The Association aims to encourage carers to recognise their own needs, to develop appropriate support for carers, to provide information and advice for carers in England, Scotland, Wales and Northern Ireland, and to bring the needs of carers to the attention of policymakers. It publishes 24 information leaflets covering relevant issues such as benefits and services. A bi-monthly journal is available by subscription, currently £3 a year.

Britain's 10,000 young carers (anyone under the age of 18 who has to undertake this task) often face particular problems and often have no one they can talk to in confidence. The Carers' National Association has produced a Young Carers' Information Pack, available from head office free of charge to young carers. The pack contains lots of practical information such as where to go for help and advice; advice on benefits; a personal information sheet for recording emergency telephone numbers; key contacts and information

138

about their relative's illness and medication; and a list of voluntary organisations which provide help for young people.

Families Anonymous
Doddington and Rollo Community Association
Charlotte Despard Avenue
London SW11 5JE
Tel: 0171 498 4680 (helpline Monday–Friday 1–4pm)

A fellowship of relatives and friends of people involved in the abuse of mind-altering substances or related behavioural problems. Families Anonymous has self-help groups throughout the country which meet regularly and are as anonymous and confidential as the name suggests. The office is staffed by volunteers and funded by voluntary contributions given at meetings and by the sale of a range of literature aimed at helping members.

Manic Depression Fellowship
8–10 High Street
Kingston-upon-Thames
Surrey KT1 1EY
Tel: 0181 974 6550

A national voluntary organisation providing support, advice and information to sufferers, their relatives, friends and others who care. The Fellowship supplies details of local self-help groups and open meetings, produces a publications list and runs a pen-friendship scheme. Members receive the regular quarterly newsletter *Pendulum*.

National Schizophrenia Fellowship
NSF National Office
28 Castle Street
Kingston-upon-Thames
Surrey KT1 1SS
Tel: 0181 547 3937 (general office). Advice line 0181 974 6814
(Monday–Friday 10–3pm.) Regional numbers are given below.

A national voluntary organisation which supports men and

women with a severe mental illness, also their families and carers. The NSF campaigns to spread a greater understanding of the problems surrounding mental illness, and to improve opportunities for people with personal experience of these problems. They will provide callers with a free information pack and put them in touch with their local or nearest support group. The NSF is often seen as the organisation which speaks for carers of people with mental illness, although its aims are wider than this.

The NSF has over 150 local groups which provide support primarily to relatives of people suffering from schizophrenia; despite the title of the agency, this service is usually open to people affected by any serious mental illness. Some NSF branches are also involved in providing services directly, for example day care.

SIBSLINK groups offer brothers, sisters, children and friends a chance to meet regularly to discuss feelings and experiences, to exchange advice, and to provide support for each other.

For details of any of these services please contact your nearest NSF regional office direct:

NSF London Region
Station House
150 Waterloo Road
London SE1 8SB
Tel: 0171 928 7668

NSF Northern England
25a Outram Street
Sutton-in-Ashfield
Notts NG17 4BA
Tel: 01623 551338

NSF Eastern England
19 Sturton Street
Cambridge CB1 2QG
Tel: 01223 303177

NSF Southern England
17 Oxford Street
Southampton SO1 1DJ
Tel: 01703 225664

NSF South East England
Maidstone Community
Support Centre
Marsham Street
Maidstone
Kent ME14 1HH
Tel: 01622 661655

NSF South West England
94 Sidwell Street
Exeter EX4 6PH
Tel: 01392 494393

NSF Midlands Region
9 St Michaels Court
Victoria Street
West Bromwich B70 8EZ
Tel: 0121 500 5988

NSF Wales
Pen-y-Fai Hospital
Bridgend
Mid-Glamorgan CG31 4LN
Tel: 01656 766330

Northern Ireland
37–39 Queen Street
Belfast BT1 6EA
Tel: 01232 248006

National Schizophrenia Fellowship (Scotland)
Shandwick Place
Edinburgh
Lothian EH2 4RT
Tel: 0131 226 2025

Provides support similar to that of the NSF (to which they are affiliated) to people with mental illness and their carers who live in Scotland.

Relatives' Association
5 Tavistock Place
London WC1H 9SS
Tel: 0171 916 6055/0181 201 9153

Offers advice, information and support to relatives of older people living in residential homes. It produces a regular newsletter and has a growing number of relative support groups nationwide.

10

Help for Particular Groups

**Ethnic minorities • Older people • Women • Addiction
and dependency • Children and young people**

ETHNIC MINORITIES

Discrimination causes many people from ethnic minorities
to be as disadvantaged in the mental health system as they
are in housing, employment and education. African-
Caribbean and Irish people, for example, are more likely to
be diagnosed schizophrenic, and there has been considerable
concern that ignorance of these cultures on the part of mental health professionals increases the risk of misdiagnosis for
these groups. Some Asian people, particularly women, may
be coping with emotional distress without any form of professional support. People from minority ethnic communities
have a right to expect services which are provided in a relevant, accessible and effective way. All mental health agencies,
including health, social services, voluntary and private
organisations, have a duty to ensure that their services are
non-discriminatory and equally accessible to all.

Regional MIND offices (see pp.91–3) can supply details of
mental health literature available in languages other than
English. In addition, people can contact their local social
services or MIND office for information about services
specifically for people from ethnic minority backgrounds. All

142

the services mentioned in this handbook are open to people from ethnic minorities; the organisations listed below, however, cater for particular needs or are able to point people towards specialist help.

Useful resources for members of ethnic minorities

Afro-Caribbean Mental Health Association (ACMHA)
35–37 Electric Avenue
London SW9 8JP
Tel: 0171 737 3603

Offers befriending and support services for Afro-Caribbean psychiatric patients and others of Afro-Caribbean origin with mental health problems, also their families and friends. The Association offers counselling, legal advice and housing advice and runs a Black Clients and Carers Project, which aims to empower people to make better use of services. ACMHA covers the London boroughs of Lambeth, Lewisham and Southwark.

Asian Family Counselling Service (Head Office)
74 The Avenue
London W13 8LB
Tel: 0181 997 5749

Provides a general, crisis and marriage counselling service to members of the Asian community. Self-referrals are accepted from any Asian person by telephone, visit or letter. Counselling is offered in Punjabi, Bengali, Urdu and Hindi. Fees are on a sliding scale, depending on income. Some telephone counselling is also available.

Chinese Mental Health Association
Oxford House
Derbyshire Street
London E2 6NG
Tel: 0171 613 1008

Aims to provide direct services such as counselling, advocacy and befriending Chinese people living in London who experience mental distress. A telephone advice service is available for people living elsewhere in the UK.

Confederation of Indian Organisations (UK)
5 Westminster Bridge Road
London SE1 7XW
Tel: 0171 928 9889

An umbrella organisation for Asian voluntary groups which provides resources, advice and information in a number of areas including health, mental health, immigration and race. It aims to raise awareness of issues affecting the Asian community, including mental health, through campaigns, research and publications.

Jewish Care (Head Office)
Stuart Young House
221 Golders Green Road
NW11 9DQ
Tel: 0181 458 3282

Jewish Care is a London and South East based organisation offering a whole range of social services. These include residential and day care, homecare services, social work and group counselling. Other branches are based in Edgware, Hackney and Redbridge. Call the head office for information.

Jewish Chabad Drugs helpline
Tel: 0181 518 6470 (Monday, Tuesday, Thursday, and Sunday morning 10am–1pm

Those seeking help can call or drop in during opening hours.

Miyad Jewish Crisis Line
Helpline: 0181 203 6211 (Sunday-Thursday 12am–12pm;
Friday until 2 hours before Chabad and from one hour
afterwards.
Outside London: 0345 581999 (all callers will be charged at
the local rate).

Also applicable to young people. For information about one-
to-one counselling, call 0181 203 6311.

NAFSIYAT
Inter-cultural Therapy Centre
278 Seven Sisters Road
London N4 2HY
Tel: 0171 263 4130

Offers psychotherapy to people from black ethnic minority
groups. It has some NHS clients referred by GPs or other
mental health professionals and accepts self-referrals, with
the consent of the GP. It offers some free therapy but otherwise a sliding scale applies, depending on income.

National Black Mental Health Association
c/o The Roachford Trust Resource Centre
70 The Parade
Green Lanes
London N4 6UU
Tel: 0181 800 2039

Provides a network for black mental health organisations,
and campaigns for more resources for voluntary organisations and an increase in the involvement of black users and
carers in mental health services.

Transcultural Psychiatry Society (UK)
c/o Dr Hassan Daudjee
Edith Cavell Hospital
Peterborough PE3 6GZ
Tel: 01733 330777 ext. 5521

Provides training in mental health and race issues, organises conferences and publishes a regular newsletter for members.

OLDER PEOPLE

Many people look forward in a positive way to reaching retirement age and giving up the rat race. They may have the opportunity to pursue pastimes and interests for which there was once no time, and to cultivate new ones. For some, however, old age brings difficult changes. They may have to live on a much lower income and to cope with bereavement and loneliness, while their physical and mental health may deteriorate.

People who have had a mental illness such as schizophrenia or manic depression are likely to find that these conditions follow them into old age, although the symptoms are often less severe. Enforced isolation, caused by lack of mobility and loneliness, can lead to anxiety and depression. But perhaps most distressing of all is dementia, a progressive decline in the ability to remember, to think and to reason. The risk of dementia increases with age and occurs in approximately 20 per cent of people over the age of 80.

Many older people today belong to a generation who find it difficult to ask for help, even though they have the same rights to services as the rest of the population. Local social services can be approached to provide a wide range of support where appropriate, such as a social worker, day care, residential care, meals on wheels or home care/home help. In addition, some local authorities offer travel concessions or provide a laundry service for people who cannot manage their own laundry or are incontinent. In some areas personal alarm systems or subsidised telephone installation may be available for those who fulfil certain criteria.

Useful resources for older people

Abbeyfield Society
53 Victoria Street

St Albans
Herts AL1 3UW
Tel: 01727 857536

Provides information on local Abbeyfield supportive housing in the UK, which aims to provide a family atmosphere. Projects include housing for ethnic minority older people and 'extra care' houses for those who are frail and require personal care.

Alzheimer's Disease Society
Gordon House
10 Greencoat Place
London SW1P 1PH
Tel: 0171 306 0606

Alzheimer's Scotland Action on Dementia
8 Hill Street
Edinburgh EH2 3JZ
Tel: 0131 225 1453

Provides information about dementia and runs local support services.

Age Concern England
Astral House
1268 London Road
London SW16 4EJ
Tel: 0181 679 8000

Age Concern Wales
4th Floor
1 Cathedral Road
Cardiff CF1 9SD
Tel: 01222 371566

Age Concern Scotland
54a Fountainbridge
Edinburgh EH3 9PT
Tel: 0131 228 5656

Age Concern Northern Ireland
3 Lower Crescent
Belfast BT7 1NR
Tel: 01232 245729

Age Concern exists to promote the well-being of older people. It produces a range of books, briefings and factsheets, and runs an information service and insurance schemes. The above addresses can give details of local groups which provide services such as advice and information, day centre and befriending schemes.

Association of Crossroads Care Attendant Schemes
10 Regent Place
Rugby
Warwickshire CV21 2PN
Tel: 01788 573653

Provides details of over 230 local schemes in the UK which provide a care attendant who can come into the home to give the carer a break.

British Red Cross Society
9 Grosvenor Crescent
London SW1 7EJ
Tel: 0171 235 5454

Provides details of services available from local centres, which may include home nursing, transport, holidays and a medical equipment loan scheme.

Counsel and Care
Twyman House
16 Bonny Street
London NW1 9PG
Tel: 0171 485 1566 (Monday–Friday 10.30–4pm)

Operates a free advice service for older people covering benefits, accommodation, the arranging of help at home and sources of charitable help.

Courses for Carers of the Elderly
Latimer House
40 Hanson Street
London W1P 7DE
Tel: 0171 380 9188

Regular courses run by the Department of Psychiatry for the Elderly at London's Middlesex Hospital. The courses, which are in two parts, each two days in length, are held in London and currently cost £85 with concessions for family carers. Details are available from the above address.

Help the Aged (England, Wales and Scotland)
16–18 St James Walk
London EC1R 0BE
Tel: 0171 253 0253.
Free helpline 0800 289404 Monday–Friday 10–4pm

Help the Aged (Northern Ireland)
Lesley House
Shaftesbury Square
Belfast BT2 7DP
Tel: 01232 230666
Free helpline 0800 289404 (Monday–Friday 10–4pm)

Provides information and advice on issues of concern to older people. Details of local groups are available from the above addresses; some run day centres and Good Neighbour Schemes.

WOMEN

Women are more likely to be admitted to psychiatric hospitals than men. In 1986, 113,386 women were admitted to hospital, in comparison with 83,865 men.

There are particular mental health problems facing women. They are twice as likely as men to be labelled as suffering from depression and are two to three times more likely to be prescribed tranquillisers Women's reproductive role can lead to premenstrual syndrome, menopausal problems, baby blues, post-natal depression and so on. Women are more likely to have been sexually abused. Women are often isolated in the home and bear the strain of caring, and they are also more likely to live in poverty. Many women also still have to cope with the pressure of conforming to the traditional stereotype of femininity, including being passive, being dependent on men and putting others before themselves.

Although this image of women is being challenged, many suffer from low self-esteem and social prejudice on the grounds of gender. Because of the immense value of confiding relationships to women's sense of emotional well-being, self-help groups are seen as a major source of help. Below are national contact numbers for local self-help groups as well as other forms of assistance:

Useful resources for women

Association for Post-natal Illness
25 Jerdan Place
London SW6 1BE
Tel: 0171 386 0868 (Monday–Friday 10am–2pm)

Advice on how to deal with post-natal illness is given by mothers who have had the illness and recovered. They are backed up by medical experts. Callers are sent a form and are allocated a counsellor. There is a countrywide network of telephone and postal volunteers.

Brook Advisory Centres
153a East Street
London SE17 2SD
Tel: 0171 708 1234. Helpline: (24 hours) 0171 617 8000

There is a network of Brook Advisory Centres in England, Scotland and Northern Ireland, providing contraceptive advice, contraceptives, pregnancy testing, pregnancy counselling and counselling for sexual and emotional problems to people under 25 years of age.

CRY-SIS
BM CRY-SIS
London WC1 3XX
Tel: 0171 404 5011

A helpline and support group giving practical advice and sympathetic understanding to mothers of crying babies who feel at the end of their tether. The above number can put mothers in touch with others in the same situation and with local support groups.

MAMA (Meet-a-Mum Association)
14 Willis Road
Croydon
Surrey CRO 2XX
Tel: 0181 665 0357

A self-help group which offers friendship and support to all mothers and aims to ease the feelings of isolation and loneliness experienced by many new mums, which may lead to, or be part of, post-natal depression. The support offered may be on a one-to-one or group basis. MAMA also has a publications list.

MATCH (Mothers Apart from Their Children)
BM Problems
London WC1N 3XX

A self-help support group for mothers living apart from their children through choice, lost custody, care orders and so on. It publishes a newsletter and a contact list for mothers who want to talk to others in the same situation.

Miscarriage Association
c/o Clayton Hospital
Northgate
Wakefield
West Yorkshire WF1 3JS
Tel: 01924 200799 (helpline Monday–Friday 9am–5pm except bank holidays)

Support, help and information for women and their families who have suffered miscarriage are given by women who have also experienced this loss. An information pack and the names of local contacts and support groups are available.

National Association for Premenstrual Syndrome
PO Box 72
Sevenoaks
Kent TN13 1XQ
Tel: 01732 741709 (recorded message with details of volunteers on call Monday–Fridays, except bank holidays, 10am–10pm)

Aims to help all sufferers of PMS by giving personal advice and support, supplying information to members and working with the medical profession to alleviate suffering.

National Childbirth Trust (NCT)
Alexandra House
Oldham Terrace
London W3 6NH
Tel: 0181 992 8637

Offers information and support in pregnancy, childbirth and early parenthood and aims to enable every parent to make informed choices. The above number will put women in touch with one of approximately 380 local groups providing a variety of support services and groups which may include: natural childbirth classes, breast-feeding counsellors, postnatal support groups, baby blues groups, babysitting circles, caesarean support, miscarriage and bereavement support and neighbourhood contacts.

Rape Crisis Centre
PO Box 69
London WC1X 9NJ
Tel: 0171 916 5466 (office). Helpline (24 hours) 0171 837 1600

Offers counselling and medical and legal help to female victims of rape or sexual abuse.

Stillbirth & Neonatal Death Society (SANDS)
28 Portland Place
London W1N 4DE
Tel: 0171 436 5881

Offers advice and long-term support to newly bereaved parents (from 22 weeks of pregnancy to one or two months after birth) through a network of over 200 local self-help groups and contacts. Also provides information, leaflets and a newsletter.

Women's Aid Federation England
PO Box 391
Bristol BS99 7WS Tel: 0117 9633494 (administration).
Helpline 0117 9633542 (Monday–Friday 10am–4pm and 7–10pm)

Northern Ireland Women's Aid
129 University Street
Belfast BT7 1HP
Tel: 01232 249041 (administration)

Scottish Women's Aid
12 Torphichen Street
Edinburgh EH3 8JQ
Tel: 0131 221 0401 (helpline Monday–Friday 10am–1pm)

Welsh Women's Aid
National Office
38–48 Crwys Road
Cardiff CF2 4NN
Tel: 01222 390874 (administration)

Provides information, support and temporary refuge for abused women and their children. A recorded message is available outside the above helpline hours (or outside 9.30–4.30 if it is an administration number) advising women how to get help in an emergency.

ADDICTION AND DEPENDENCY

These are difficult habits to break. Most people who do so successfully say they benefitted from talking in confidence to a qualified person who can offer help. The first step is always the most difficult, and so initial contact is often made by telephone. It is always better for the person concerned to refer themselves, as this is the first test of motivation. Breaking habits may result in a long period of sadness and stress until the person has learnt to come to terms with this major change.

Alcohol

Many adults enjoy a drink without coming to any harm, but even at very low levels of consumption your judgement can be affected. The upper limits for sensible social drinking are:

- men: 21 units a week including two or three days without alcohol

- women: 14 units a week including two or three days without alcohol
(One unit (8g) of alcohol = ½ pint of beer or one glass of wine *or* one standard measure of spirits.)

People who continually drink above these levels run the risk of a range of physical problems including impotence and damage to the liver and brain. Excessive drinking can also lead to social and relationship problems; poor diet and self-care; an increased rate of violence, including domestic violence; and an increased risk of accidents, particularly on the road. In serious cases people feel a compulsion to drink and the body can become physically dependent on alcohol.

Alcohol and mental health

- excessive drinking is often related to depression and anxiety, either as an effect of the habit or because a person who is suffering from depression or anxiety turns to alcohol as a means of relief

154

- the risk of suicide and self-harm is much greater in people who drink excessively (see Chapter 8)

- hallucinations of vision or hearing may occur, particularly as symptoms of withdrawal from alcohol dependency

- prolonged alcohol misuse may lead to dementia (see pp. 26–27)

Help available

Medical treatment is available to help people who drink excessively to dry out. In cases of physical dependence the treatment involves stopping the consumption of alcohol and giving medication to reduce the withdrawal symptoms. Admission to hospital is often involved, although the treatment may be given at home if enough support and medical supervision are available.

In some areas, group therapy is available either in hospital or on an outpatient basis. The aim of therapy is to help boost the motivation to stay off drink, and to tackle any personal problems which might have led to the drink habit in the first place.

Antabuse and **Abstem** are drugs which can cause very unpleasant physical symptoms when alcohol is taken. They are sometimes prescribed by doctors to help people with serious and persistent alcohol problems who cannot resist the urge to drink. These drugs may also have unpleasant side-effects.

Residential care for a brief period in a specialist hostel is another option to help ex-drinkers tackle their problems and rebuild their lives. Contact your local social services department for more information.

Self-help groups can be very valuable in giving support to problem drinkers who want to stop. Contact your local social services, MIND branch or Community Health Council for details of groups in your area. Some of the larger organisations offering help with alcohol problems are listed below.

155

Useful resources for people suffering from alcohol addiction or dependency

ACCEPT Services
724 Fulham Road
London SW6 5SE
Tel: 0171 371 7477

A centre for people who want to stop drinking. The service includes groups, individual counselling and a relatives' support group. Self-referral is requested, and clients must be sober at the appointment. Anyone can be seen as there is no catchment area.

Alcoholics Anonymous
General Service Office
PO Box 1
Stonebow House
Stonebow
York YO2 2NJ
Tel: 01904 644026. Helplines (England:) 0171 352 3001
(Monday–Sunday 10am–10pm); (Scotland:) 0141 221 9027
(Monday–Friday 9am–5pm, recorded message giving
volunteer on call outside these hours); (Wales:) 01646
695555, (24 hours); (Northern Ireland:) 01232 681084
(Monday–Friday 9am–5pm)

Details of local helplines can be obtained from the above numbers or found in local telephone directories. There is also a network of local groups.

Alcohol Concern
Waterbridge House
32–36 Loman Street
London SE1 0EE
Tel: 0171 928 7377

Alcohol Concern Wales
4 Dock Chambers
Bute Street

Cardiff CF1 6AG
Tel: 01222 488000

Scottish Council on Alcohol
137–145 Sauchiehall Street
Glasgow G2 3EW
Tel: 0141 333 9677

Northern Ireland Council on Alcohol
40 Elmwood Avenue
Belfast BT9 6AZ
Tel: 01232 664434

These national agencies are concerned with alcohol abuse and provide information, magazines and leaflets. They also run the Alcohol Services Directory and can put people in touch with local support.

Al-Anon Family Groups
61 Great Dover Street
London SE1 4YF
Tel: 0171 403 0888 (24-hour confidential helpline)

Helps families and friends of problem drinkers. Alateen, part of Al-Anon, is for teenagers who are affected by someone else's drinking.

Drinkline (The National Alcohol Helpline)
13–14 West Smithfield
London EC1A 9DH
Tel: 0171 332 0150 (administration). Helpline 0171 332 0202 (Monday–Friday 9.30–11pm, Saturday and Sunday 6–11pm); London Area Number: 0171 332 0202; rest of UK: 01345 320202; Dial and Listen Alcohol Information Tapes: Freephone 0500 801802.

Provides advice and information to callers who are worried about their own or someone else's drinking. It can also give details of local support.

157

Drug misuse

The illegal use of non-prescribed drugs has become increasingly common, particularly amongst young people. A wide variety of potentially harmful substances are available including heroin, barbiturates, benzodiazepines, cocaine, ecstasy, amphetamines, LSD, solvents and 'magic mushrooms'.

Apart from the temporary effects for which these drugs are taken, their use can lead to more serious and long-lasting problems. Some drugs such as heroin are addictive, and people may need medical treatment if they want to come off them. As with treatment for alcohol dependence, it may involve taking medication under close medical supervision for withdrawal symptoms. Psychological dependence also has to be tackled and individual or group therapy, or a brief time in residential care, may be helpful. Each area in the UK has a team to advise and help drug misusers, whether they want to stop taking drugs or need help with some other drug-related problem (see SCODA entry on p. 160).

Certain drugs, particularly hallucinogenic ones like LSD, can cause frightening experiences either at the time they are taken or in flashbacks. Occasionally, prolonged use of drugs is followed by persistent psychotic symptoms which need psychiatric treatment. Whether drugs can trigger a permanent serious mental illness in vulnerable people is uncertain, although common sense suggests that people with mental health problems should avoid the risk.

Useful resources for people suffering from drug addiction or dependency

ADFAM (Aid for Addicts and Families)
18 Hatton Place
London EC1N 8ND
Tel: 0171 405 3923 (helpline Monday–Friday 10am–5pm)

Offers confidential telephone support and advice for people with illegal or prescribed drug problems, and for their families. It also provides training and organises projects working with the families of drug-users.

CITA (Council for Involuntary Tranquilliser Addiction)
Cavendish House
Brighton Road
Waterloo
Liverpool L22 5NG
Tel: 0151 928 4632/474 9626 (administration). Helpline 0151 949 0102 (Monday–Friday 9.30–5pm, ansaphone outside these hours)

A national organisation established to raise awareness of the problems associated with tranquilliser addiction.

Families Anonymous
Unit 37
Doddington and Rollo Community Association
Charlotte Despard Avenue
London SW11 5JE
Tel: 0171 498 4680

A network of self-help support groups for families and friends of those with a drug problem or behaviour problems related to the taking of drugs.

Freephone Drug Problems
Dial 100 and ask for Freephone Drug Problems, which gives details of local help and numbers for Scotland, Wales and Ireland.

Narcotics Anonymous
PO Box 1980
London N19 3LS
Tel: 0171 272 9040 (administration). Helpline 0171 498 9005 (daily 10am–8pm, ansaphone outside these hours.) Tape giving details of groups in the London area: 0171 281 9933.

A self-help group of recovering addicts who meet regularly to help each other stay clean. The helpline offers confidential help, support and details of local meetings to anyone who wants to stop using drugs.

RELEASE
388 Old Street
London EC1V 9LT
Tel: 0171 729 9904 (adviceline Monday–Friday 10am–6pm)
Emergency helpline 0171 603 8654 (24-hour)

Offers advice, information and referral on legal and drug-related problems for users, families and friends.

Re-Solv (Society for the Prevention of Solvent and Volatile Substance Abuse)
30A High Street
Stone
Staffordshire ST15 8AW
Tel: 01785 817885

Publishes booklets and videos about solvent abuse. It can also supply information on useful local agencies.

SCODA (Standing Conference on Drug Abuse)
Waterbridge House
32–36 Loman Street
London SE1 0EE
Tel: 0171 928 9500

Does not give direct support to callers but supplies information about local drug advice agencies.

Turning Point
New Loom House
101 Back Church Lane
London E1 1LU
Tel: 0171 702 2300

Over 45 projects offer residential rehabilitation, day care and street level advice to people with drink, drug and mental health problems.

Other addictions

GAMBLING

GamAnon
PO Box 88
London SW10 0EU
Tel: 0181 741 4181 (24-hour helpline)

An organisation for the families and close friends of compulsive gamblers which offers understanding, friendship and practical help.

Gamblers Anonymous
PO Box 88
London SW10 0EU
Tel: 0181 741 4181 (24-hour helpline)

A self-help group of men and women who share a problem with gambling.

Gamblers Anonymous and GamAnon share the same address, and by ringing the above number callers will be referred to the relevant duty volunteer who can offer telephone support as well as details of local meetings.

SMOKING

ASH UK (Action on Smoking and Health)
109 Gloucester Place
London W1H 3PH
Tel: 0171 935 3519

Can offer all sorts of information and advice on all aspects of smoking including ways of breaking the habit.

ASH Scotland
8 Frederick Street
Edinburgh EH2 2HB
Tel: 0131 225 4725 (administration). Helpline 0131 226 5999 (Monday–Friday 9am–5pm)

QUIT
102 Gloucester Place
London W1H 3DA
Tel: 0171 487 3000 (helpline Monday–Friday
9.30am–5.30pm, ansaphone outside these hours)

Aims to help people stop smoking. As well as telephone advice and counselling the above number may be able to put callers in touch with a local support group.

Smokeline
Tel: 0800 848484

A free information and counselling service for people in Scotland who want support and advice to quite smoking.

Northern Ireland helpline 01232 663281
Welsh helpline 01222 641888

These helplines give information, advice and support to people who need help to stop smoking.

CHILDREN AND YOUNG PEOPLE

Childhood and adolescence are meant to be happy times, but this is certainly not so for everyone. During these important stages young people's physical, intellectual and emotional development is rapid and continuously changing. It is also a time when they may be experiencing bullying or other forms of pressure at school, and unhappy relationships at home (including sexually, physically or emotionally abusive ones). In addition the family may move, there may be problems with girlfriends or boyfriends, and they may go through a bereavement or their parents' divorce.

Emotional and behavioural problems in childhood and adolescence are common and can usually be dealt with by reassurance and tackling the causes if they are known. But sometimes the problems and experiences can be very distressing and lead to depression which in young people should never be ignored or swept under the carpet. Not only are the mental health and potential of the young person at stake, but a distressed or disturbed child can disturb the well-being of their family or community. If there is persistent unhappiness, coupled with a feeling that life will never get better, the cause must be carefully explored and help given.

Mental health problems in later life, such as eating disorders and conditions related to depression and anxiety, sometimes began when the sufferer is young. Even serious mental illness such as manic depression and schizophrenia can start during adolescence, with similar symptoms to those occurring in adults (see Chapter 1). Attempted suicide, and indeed suicide rates amongst young people, also seem to be rising.

Help available

Specialist assessment and help may be available from child guidance clinics, where multi-disciplinary teams including child psychiatrists, psychotherapists, counsellors, psychologists, social workers and other professionals work together with the child or young person and their family. GPs or social workers can refer, although some child guidance clinics accept referrals from parents.

Educational psychologists may also be able to help and can usually be contacted through schools, local education departments or GPs. They are trained to work with children and have a special understanding of their emotional and intellectual development.

Very occasionally, hospital admission is needed for assessment or treatment. There are some specialist hospital facilities for young people but these are scarce and it sometimes means admission to an adult ward, which is far from ideal. There is no lower age limit in the application of the Mental Health Act 1983, so in theory a child or young person who is really disturbed can be treated or compulsorily detained under the Act. However, in practice children are seldom detained and are either admitted to hospital as informal patients by their parents or treated in other settings.

163

Useful resources for children and young people

Advice, Advocacy and Representation Service for Children
1 Sickle Street
Manchester M60 2AA
Tel: 0161 839 8442 (administration). Helpline 0800 616101
(daily–10pm)

Provides a confidential advocacy service for any child or young person who wants their wishes and feelings to be heard and represented. The main focus of ASC's work is young people in care.

Anti-Bullying Campaign
10 Borough High Street
London SE1 9QO
Tel: 0171 378 1446 (helpline Monday–Friday 9.30am–5pm)

Helps parents to work with schools to combat the problem of bullying. Parents' information packs are available for £2 and schools' resource packs for £8 from the above address.

Brook Advisory Centres
153A East Street
London SE17 2SD
Tel: 0171 708 1234. Helpline 0171 617 8000 (24 hours)

A network of centres in Northern Ireland, Scotland and England (though not in Wales) provide contraceptive advice, contraceptives, pregnancy testing, pregnancy counselling and counselling for sexual and emotional problems for young people under the age of 25.

Child and Family Department
Tavistock Clinic
120 Belsize Lane
London NW3 5BA
Tel: 0171 435 7111

The Child and Family Department is part of the Tavistock Clinic, which is an NHS outpatients facility. It offers a multidisciplinary approach to children and young people experiencing difficulties with their mental or emotional health. Consultation and treatment are available for the young person, their parents and families. Parents and professionals may refer by telephone or letter, contacting the Intake Secretary at the address or number above.

Childline
2nd Floor
Royal Main Building
Studd Street
London N1 0QW
Helpline: 0800 1111 (24 hours, every day of the year.)

Childline (Scotland)
33 Stockwell Street
Glasgow G1 4BR
Helpline: 0800 1111 (24 hours, every day of the year)

A free national helpline offering confidential counselling to children in trouble or danger in any part of the UK. They also provide advice by letter.

Council for Wales of Voluntary Youth Services
Llys Leslie
Lon-y-Llyn
Caerphilly CF8 1BQ
Tel: 01222 880088

National umbrella organisation for Wales which directs callers to a wide range of local leisure and educational youth facilities.

Eating Disorders Association
Sackville Place
44 Magdalen Street
Norwich

Norfolk NR3 1JU
Tel: 01603 765050 (youth helpline Monday, Tuesday and
Wednesday 4–6pm)

Helpline is for young people under the age of 18 who want
to talk to someone about their eating problems.

Hyperactive Children's Support Group (HCSG)
71 Whyte Lane
Chichester
Sussex PO19 2LD

Aims to help and support hyperactive children and their
parents. It provides information about the causes of hyper-
activity and the help available.

National Council for Voluntary Youth Services
Coborn House
3 Coborn Road
London E3 2DA
Tel: 0181 980 5712

National umbrella organisation for England which directs
callers to a wide range of local leisure and educational youth
facilities.

Parentline
Westbury House
57 Hart Road
Thundersley
Essex SS7 3PD
Tel: 01268 757077

Has a network of 27 regional telephone helplines for parents
under stress, run by trained volunteers who are themselves
parents.

Standing Scottish Conference of Voluntary Youth Organisations
Central Hall
West Tolcross
Edinburgh EH3 9BP
Tel: 0131 229 0339

National umbrella organisation for Scotland which directs callers to a wide range of local leisure and educational youth facilities.

Young Minds
22A Boston Place
London NW1 6ER
Tel: 0171 724 7262. Helpline 01345 626376 (Monday–Friday 9am–5pm.) At present this is only a pilot line available in Yorkshire and Humberside. It is designed for concerned adults who want to speak to a mental health professional about the feelings or emotions of a young person they know or look after.

The national association for child and family mental health, it was set up to raise awareness of the emotional and behavioural problems of children and young people and to inform the public about the more common problems and the help available. Members receive a quarterly newsletter.

Details of local services are available from the above address and the information service produces a range of leaflets including: *How Can Child Psychotherapists Help?*; *What Are Child and Family Consultation Services (or Child Guidance Centres)?*; *Bullying – Why it matters*; *Why Do Young Minds Matter?*; *How Can Psychologists Help Children?*; *The Difference between Growing Pains and Signs of Trouble*; *How Can Family Therapy Help my Family?*; *Children and Young People Get Depressed Too*; *Worried about a Young Person's Eating Problems?*

167

Youth Access
Magazine Business Centre
11 Newark Street
Leicester LE1 5SS
Tel: 0116 2558763

Can give contacts for local counselling, advice and information services for young people in England, Wales, Scotland and Northern Ireland.

Youthnet
Lamont House
Purdy's Lane
Saintfield Road
Belfast BT8 4TA
Tel: 01232 643882

National umbrella organisation for Northern Ireland which directs callers to a wide range of local leisure and educational facilities.

11

Your Rights

WHY RIGHTS ARE IMPORTANT

This chapter describes the various rights which people have as users of services, patients, carers and relatives. Mental health problems often lead to a loss of confidence, and it is all too easy to forget about your rights and to accept unquestioningly everything that professionals say. There are strong pressures on patients to conform, to accept treatment in a passive way, and it can be very difficult to question diagnosis, treatment and other professional advice or decisions. But encouraging a submissive attitude is misguided, as it will not help professionals to give the best service based on a real understanding of the person, and it will not help them to recognise their mistakes and learn from them. And for the patients, knowing your rights and being able to assert your needs and wishes goes hand in hand with good mental health and being in control of your own life. It will boost your confidence, which is not only therapeutic in itself but can also improve the outcome of a consultation with a doctor or other professional.

169

YOUR RIGHT TO SERVICES

As a user of mental health services you have a right to expect the health service and the local authority social services to provide care and treatment which meet your needs. The question of rights to services is quite complicated. The law gives health and local authorities the **power** to arrange for a wide range of different services, but their **duties** under the law are much narrower. Even where there is a duty to provide a particular service, this usually depends on a doctor, social worker or other professional agreeing that it is necessary. Apart from the law of the land, there are also a variety of codes of practice and written policies which give guidance to professionals about what they should and should not do. Some of these give significant rights to users of services, although not legal rights.

Under the National Health Service and Community Care Act 1990, the right to services hinges on your needs, as assessed by a professional. If you are in agreement about what the needs are with the professional doing the assessment, you can go on to discuss the kind of help which should be provided. Professionals have a duty to listen to your views about your needs, and how they should be met. If there is disagreement, you have a right to complain and to ask for decisions to be reviewed. There is also a fundamental right under the Race Relations Act 1976 and the Sex Discrimination Act 1975 not to be discriminated against, and for everyone, whatever their sex, marital status, race, colour, nationality or ethnic origin, to have equal access to effective services.

Rights to health care

If you have a mental illness or other mental disorder, you have a right to the services of a GP, and through your GP the right to specialist psychiatric services. You can ask your doctor to refer you to a consultant psychiatrist, if the doctor thinks it is necessary. You may also ask your GP or psychiatrist to refer you for a second opinion to another psychiatrist (again, this is not an absolute right and the doctor has discretion). Your GP or psychiatrist is responsible for arranging treatment. This is usually provided locally, but if you have special requirements the doctor may arrange for you to be seen at an appropriate hospital or clinic further afield. In an emergency you are entitled to receive necessary medical care from your GP or through the hospital accident and emergency service, and from the ambulance service.

Hospital treatment as an inpatient may be provided if your doctor decides it is necessary. While decisions about admission and discharge rest with the consultant psychiatrist, a Department of Health Circular called *The Care Programme Approach*, published in 1990, directs that 'if a patient's minimum needs for treatment in the community cannot be met, in-patient treatment should be offered or continued'.

The Patient's Charter

This is a government scheme spelling out patients' rights and the standards of service you are entitled to expect. Under the Charter you are given additional rights to information about health service quality standards and maximum waiting times. It sets out various standards to be aimed for, which include the following:

- you will be treated with respect for privacy, dignity, and religious and cultural beliefs
- when you attend an outpatient clinic, you will be given a specific appointment time and will be seen within 30 minutes of it
- a named nurse will be responsible for your nursing care
- before you are discharged from hospital a decision should be made about any continuing health or social care needs you may have

Rights to community care

Under the National Health Service and Community Care Act 1990, the local authority social services have a legal duty

171

to assess the community care needs of people with mental health problems. They also have a duty to make sure that a range of other services are available for people whom they assess as being in need. These include:

- day care
- supported housing
- help in the home
- meals-on-wheels
- travel permits
- help with holidays

The services offered to you will depend on the assessment of individual need made by professionals, and may be provided directly by the social services (through their social workers, day centres and hostels), by the health service, or by voluntary or private organisations. Health and social services should work in a coordinated way to provide the necessary care.

Rights to aftercare

Under Section 117 of the Mental Health Act, if you are being discharged from a treatment order (Section 3) or a hospital order made by the courts (Section 37) you have a legal right to aftercare. All local health and social services have to make sure that people's aftercare needs are properly assessed and planned for before they leave hospital, and are then regularly reviewed. This should be done with your involvement and agreement; Section 117 aftercare is voluntary for patients, but it is compulsory for the health and social services to try to provide it.

The Care Programme Approach

Under the 1990 government circular *The Care Programme Approach*, all health authorities are directed to ensure that people referred to the specialist psychiatric services receive a proper level of service. People's needs must be properly

172

assessed, and professionals should then work closely with patients and carers in agreeing a care plan which is reviewed regularly. In some ways this is an important extension of the rights to aftercare under Section 117, although it applies to all psychiatric patients whatever their problems and in some places it is implemented in such a general way that it has little impact. Each area should have its own local policy, information about which should be available to users of services and their families. (See pp. 65–66 for more details of Section 117 and *The Care Programme Approach*.)

Access to records

Health and social services staff keep records of various kinds. These include:

- medical notes held by the GP
- written medical records kept on each patient who attends hospital as an inpatient or outpatient
- nursing notes kept as part of the hospital record, or held separately by a community psychiatric nurse
- social services case files held by a social worker
- other written records held by day centres or residential establishments
- computer records held by health and social services

All these records are confidential, and information about you should not be passed without your permission to any person who is not on the staff of the agency concerned.

You have a right to see any written health records about you which were produced after November 1991, and any social services records about you. Simply ask for an appointment to view them. If you disagree with anything you can ask for the record to be corrected by agreement, or to have your disagreement recorded. With both medical and social services records, you will not be able to see any information from or about third parties without their permission. A senior professional may also decide that you should not see records if the content is thought damaging to your health.

You can ask if any part of the records are being withheld, and for an explanation. The Data Protection Act 1984 gives people the right of access to all records held about them on computer.

Mental health professionals are increasingly keen to involve people in planning their own care and are more amenable than they used to be to sharing written records and care plans. It is now widely seen as good practice for the person concerned not only to be involved in care plans and written reviews, but also to receive copies of these documents.

Your right to have your voice heard

Users and ex-users of services have first-hand experience and an understanding of the whole mental health system that policy-makers and service planners should be tapping. The NHS and Community Care Act 1990 and various other government guidelines in fact make it a duty for health and social services to consult with users and carers about the services which they provide or arrange. In many parts of the country, local health and social services and voluntary agencies have set up systems to ensure that users and carers are consulted. But elsewhere, unfortunately, this is done in a tokenistic way through a small number of individuals or through a voluntary organisation which is asked to speak for users' views.

For details of your own local arrangements, contact your health agency or social services, or else the local branch of MIND or the National Schizophrenia Fellowship.

YOUR RIGHTS AS A PATIENT

If you are what is called an 'informal' hospital patient you are in hospital on a voluntary basis, or at least you have not objected to being in hospital; you are free to leave or to refuse treatment whenever you wish. If you are detained under a section of the Mental Health Act (see pp. 114–16) you may lawfully be held in hospital against your will, but you still have certain rights. The main ones are described below.

The right to refuse treatment

You may refuse treatment altogether if you are detained under Sections 4, 5, 135 or 136 of the Mental Health Act. If you are on a Section 3, you have the right to refuse drug treatment after three months. You cannot then be compelled to undergo further treatment unless an outside psychiatrist appointed by the Mental Health Act Commission interviews you and agrees that your treatment should continue. If you are detained under any section you may refuse electro-convulsive therapy unless an outside psychiatrist appointed by the Mental Health Act Commission interviews you and agrees it is necessary.

You may be given treatment against your will in an emergency where immediate action is necessary to save life or to prevent serious and immediate danger to yourself or others. This comes under Section 62 of the Mental Health Act (see pp. 52–3).

The right to appeal against detention

If you want to leave hospital you should start by discussing the matter with your psychiatrist, who can discharge you, and with your nearest relative, who is entitled to order your discharge (see p. 181). You also have the right, however, to appeal against detention in hospital to the Mental Health Review Tribunal. The Tribunal consists of a lawyer (who chairs it), a specially appointed psychiatrist not connected with the local service, and a lay person who has relevant knowledge or experience. The Tribunal will hear your case and has the power to order your discharge. You have the right to be present at the hearing and to be legally represented, and also to ask for a report from an independent

175

doctor. You may be able to get Legal Aid to cover the cost of legal representation and of any independent reports (a solicitor, Citizens' Advice Bureau or local law centre will help you work out if you are eligible).

Your rights to appeal are as follows (see pp. 114–16 for an explanation of the various Sections of the Mental Health Act referred to):

- **Sections 4, 5, 135, 136:** there is no right of appeal in these short-term sections

- **Section 2:** you may appeal within 14 days of your detention

- **Sections 3 and 7:** you may appeal once in the period of up to six months during which the Section is in force; if your Section is renewed you may appeal once within the second six-month period, and then once each year after that

- **Section 37:** if you are detained under a Hospital or Guardianship Order made by a criminal court, you have similar rights of appeal to those of people held under Sections 3 and 7, but **not** for the first six months. Your initial rights of appeal are likely to be through the court system; if you need information you should ask hospital staff, and you may need to consult a solicitor. The nearest relative has no right to order the discharge of Section 37 orders, but after the first six months may appeal to the Tribunal on behalf of the patient

If you do not apply to the Tribunal yourself, your case will automatically be referred to the Tribunal after six months if you are on a Section 3, and then every three years (or every year if you are under the age of 16). If you are on a Section 37 Hospital Order made by the courts, your case will automatically be referred after three years.

HOW TO APPEAL

Tell the hospital staff you wish to appeal to the Tribunal. They have a legal duty to arrange for you to be given information and help in this connection.

MENTAL HEALTH REVIEW TRIBUNAL OFFICES

**North Thames
East Anglia and Oxford
Regional Health Authorities**
Block 1, Spur 5
Canons Park Government
Buildings ,
Honeypot Lane
Stanmore HA7 1AY
Tel: 0171 972 2000

**S.W. Thames, S.E. Thames,
Wessex and South-Western
Regional Health Authorities**
Block 3, Crown Offices,
Kingston ByPass Road
Surbiton
Surrey KT6 5QN

Tel: 0181 398 4166

**Northern Yorkshire and
Trent Regional Authorities**
Spur A, Block 5
Government Buildings
Chalfont House
Western Boulevard
Nottingham NG8 3RZ
Tel: 0115 9294222

**North-Western Mersey
and West Midlands Regional
Health Authorities**
3rd Floor, Cressingham
House
249 St Mary's Road L19 0NF
Liverpool L19 0NF
Tel: 0151 494 0095

Wales
1st Floor, New Crown Buildings
Cathays Park
Cardiff CF1 3NQ
Tel: 01222 825328

Northern Ireland
Room 112B, Dundonald
House
Upper Newtownards
Belfast BT4 3SF
Tel: 01232 485550

Scotland: appeals are made through the local Sheriff's Court.

Hospital managers' reviews

The hospital managers, represented by a panel of lay people including members of the health authority or NHS trust, also have the power to discharge patients from their Section, and any detained patient may apply to the hospital managers for his or her case to be reviewed. Strictly speaking this is not a formal appeal, although in practice it is a similar process: the managers interview the patient, look at case notes, consider the view of the psychiatrist and other professionals, and decide whether or not to discharge you.

The right to information

When you are admitted to hospital under a Section of the Mental Health Act, the hospital staff have a duty to inform you about the Section you are being detained under. They must also inform you of your rights of appeal to a Mental Health Review Tribunal and to apply to the hospital managers. This information must be given to you in writing, and explained to you, as soon as possible after your detention.

The hospital also has a duty to give the same information to your nearest relative, and to give them notice of your discharge from hospital. If you do not want your nearest relative to be informed by the hospital, you have the right to request that this information is not given. However, the approved social worker has an absolute duty to inform your nearest relative of your *admission*; the social worker also has a duty to inform the nearest relative of that relative's powers of discharge, and you as the patient cannot prevent this information from being given.

OTHER CIVIL RIGHTS

Voting Rights

Mental illness does not in itself disqualify people from voting in parliamentary or local elections. As long as you are on the register of electors, and you are capable of identifying yourself and discriminating between the candidates, you are entitled to vote. The presiding officer at the polling station may ask you some specific questions if in doubt about your capacity to understand; e.g. 'Are you the person registered in the register of parliamentary electors?' If you cannot answer these questions you may be prevented from voting. Your right to vote is not affected by being in hospital, although there are some restrictions on people registering to vote while hospital patients – informal patients may register if they are able to make a declaration on a special form to an authorised member of hospital staff; detained patients cannot register as electors.

The right to stand for public office

Under common law, a person with a mental illness may be disqualified from being an MP during 'non-lucid intervals'. No such disqualification exists for the House of Lords or for elected members of local councils.

Jury service

A person is disqualified from jury service if he or she is currently receiving in-patient or out-patient medical treatment for mental illness.

Marriage

Anyone, including a detained patient, is allowed to marry as long as he or she is capable of understanding the duties and responsibilities of marriage.

Employment

As yet there is no effective law to protect mentally ill people against discrimination in employment. Grounds for dismissal would be where a person is incapable of performing the job, or fails to answer questions about health truthfully. An employer wishing to dismiss an employee because he or she is incapable due to illness must take steps to obtain a medical assessment either from the employee's GP, with their consent, or from another doctor. (See also Chapter 13).

Driving

Mental illness does not normally count as one of the disabilities which have to be notified to the DVLC. Occasionally, however, driving ability is affected and DVLC be informed. This may lead to a driving licence being withdrawn. If this happens there is a right of appeal through the magistrates' courts.

YOUR RIGHTS AS A CARER

Carers have a right to expect mental health professionals to listen to them and consider their views, and to involve them in planning wherever carers are making a significant contribution to the support of the person concerned. The Mental Health Act Code of Practice 1993 makes it clear that professionals must listen to carers' views when making assessments under the Act. Other government circulars such as *The Care Programme Approach* (1990) also emphasise the importance of involving carers. However, professionals are sometimes asked by patients not to share information with carers; in such instances the professionals would be bound by a duty of confidentiality. When this happens it can be frustrating and upsetting, but the professional team still have to consider the position of carers, who should at least expect to be able to put forward their views, and to receive some advice and support in their own right.

YOUR RIGHTS AS A NEAREST RELATIVE

The Mental Health Act creates a special role for the 'nearest relative' of a person with a mental disorder. A definition of the nearest relative, and an explanation of the role they play, are on pp. 134–36. Your main rights as a nearest relative are as follows:

• you may ask for an approved social worker to arrange for a formal mental health assessment (see p. 113), and to be informed in writing of the reason if no application for hospital admission is then made

• you yourself may apply for your relative to be admitted to

hospital, based on the recommendations of two doctors –
or one in an emergency (but note that the preferred applicant is normally the approved social worker)

- you have the right to be consulted if your relative is being
  assessed under the Mental Health Act. You may also prevent an application for a treatment order (Section 3) or
  guardianship being made by withholding your consent

- you may order the discharge of your relative from hospital
  under Sections 2 or 3, giving 72 hours' notice in writing.
  This may be over-ruled by the psychiatrist if he or she con-
  siders that the person is a danger to themselves or others.
  If the psychiatrist over-rules you, you can appeal to the
  Mental Health Review Tribunal

- under Section 7 you have the right to discharge your relative from guardianship

- you have the right to information from an approved social
  worker about your role as nearest relative and your right
  to discharge your relative

- you have the right to information from the hospital about
  the effect of detention under the Act, and rights of appeal.
  You also have the right to be informed by the hospital
  about your relative being discharged from hospital, and to
  be given seven days' notice if practicable. The patient may,
  however, ask the hospital not to give you this information

When you exercise your rights as nearest relative it is
assumed that you yourself are mentally competent, and that
you are acting in a reasonable way which takes account of
the welfare of the patient and the interests of the public. If
this is in dispute, your rights as nearest relative may be
assigned to someone else by the county court. If you do not
want to act as nearest relative, you may agree with another
suitable person for them to take on the role (contact your
local social services for advice).

ADVOCACY

It is not always easy to speak up and assert your rights and needs as a user of mental health services. Users and their families often feel in a less powerful position than the professionals working with them, and in danger of not being listened to. Worse still is the fear that raising concerns may elicit a defensive response, or even set up personal conflicts which could undermine the assistance that is needed. It is therefore often helpful to get the support of another person, who can act as an advocate and get the message across.

Advocacy has become widely accepted by health and social services and voluntary organisations as a way of helping people to secure their rights and get the services they want and need. Professionals are now increasingly involving users and carers in meetings and discussions about their needs, a process which they see as an essential element in mental health care and treatment (if they do not, challenge them).

The aim of advocacy is to empower users, not to let other people take over. Relatives and friends are often able to give support and can take on an informal advocacy role provided their interests are not in conflict. There are also a growing number of formal schemes throughout the country, most of which fall into one or other of the following categories:

- **citizen advocacy**: an unpaid volunteer usually with some training and support from a voluntary organisation, helps and supports the user

- **professional advocacy**: a paid advocate, with training and support from an organisation which is independent of those who are providing services to the user, provides support

- **self-advocacy**: the user represents him/herself, supported by a group of fellow users

- **legal advocacy**: this may be provided by a solicitor or law centre in relation to the legal rights of users; in some circumstances a lawyer may be involved in formally representing the interests of a user in court proceedings or at a Mental Health Review Tribunal (see p. 177)

To find out about any advocacy schemes in your area, contact the local branch of MIND or a Citizens' Advice Bureau.

Working with an advocate

The role of an advocate is to support the user, and to act in accordance with their wishes. A relationship of trust between them is therefore important, and the advocate should take whatever time is needed to establish it. The advocate should only speak or act with the user's permission, however frustrating this may be if the user is reluctant to raise issues. To be effective, the advocate must be independent of any other agencies working with the user so as to avoid conflict of interest. The advocate must also observe strict confidentiality and never pass on information without permission. Abiding by these ground rules an advocate may be a powerful ally in various situations such as:

- helping a user to get access to a service
- challenging a decision, e.g. to withhold a service
- helping a user to express their views in meetings with professionals, for example hospital ward rounds or review meetings in establishments.

Mental health professionals as advocates

Professionals such as community psychiatric nurses and social workers sometimes see themselves as advocates for their clients/patients, but there are drawbacks and limitations. They may indeed be able to represent users in communicating with another agency, but they cannot be independent and objective in relation to their own work. Although all professionals should consult with patients and discuss their views to make sure they are providing the right help, this is not the same as advocacy, because professionals are bound by the policies and financial restrictions of their

THE MENTAL HEALTH HANDBOOK

employers. Similar strictures can apply to voluntary organisations especially now they are increasingly involved in providing services to people and are often dependent on health or social services for their funding. Their traditional role in providing advocacy for users and their families may therefore be compromised.

User organisations

There are a number of organisations run by users for users. To find out if there is a user group in your area, contact your local branch of MIND, or national networks such as the UK Advocacy Network, MINDLINK or Survivors Speak Out. Further details of these organisations can be found on pp. 87–89.

COMPLAINTS

The professionals who provide the mental health services described in this book generally try hard to do a good job and listen to your point of view. However, things can go wrong or you may disagree with them. If so, start by discussing the issue with the person concerned. If this does not resolve the problem and you are still not satisfied, you should consider making a complaint. It may help to talk the problem over with an independent person first, for example through the local branch of MIND (see pp. 91–3) or the National Schizophrenia Fellowship (see pp. 140–2); they may offer help and support and refer you to an advocacy service (see above). You can complain either about a service, or about the lack of a service.

Who should you complain to?

This depends on who is responsible for the service you are complaining about, and whether they have a formal complaints procedure. Health and social services are required to have such procedures and to give you information about them. Many voluntary organisations now have similar policies.

Social services

For the social services or social work department, or other local authority departments such as housing, the complaints procedure will be broadly as follows:

- **stage 1**: talk to the staff who are providing the service you are complaining about, and try to sort the problems out

- **stage 2**: if you are not satisfied, or if you feel you cannot talk to the staff concerned, ask to talk to the manager who should look into the problem for you

- **stage 3**: if you are still not satisfied, put your complaint in writing, and send it to the complaints manager or to the director of the department. Ask to have your complaint investigated

- **stage 4**: some complaints procedures have another stage which allows you to appeal to a panel of people who are independent of earlier decisions

Your local councillor

As well as going through the complaints procedure, you are also entitled to contact your local councillor about any council service. Councillors are ultimately responsible for services in their area. If your complaint is about the lack of a service, your councillor may be the best person to contact. You could also contact the councillor who chairs the relevant committee, such as the social services committee. You can find out the name of your local councillor by contacting the local library or any council office.

Hospital and psychiatric services

The local health service is likely to have a complaints procedure similar to the one outlined above. If your complaint is about your treatment, ask to make an appointment to see the consultant. If it concerns the nursing service, ask to see the senior nurse manager. If you are not satisfied, put your complaint in writing to the complaints manager or the chief executive of the hospital or health authority. Local Community Health Councils also offer advice and practical help to people wishing to make a complaint about any health service, including GPs.

General practitioners (GPs)

If you have a complaint about a service from your GP which cannot be resolved by discussion with him or her, you can write to the Family Health Service Authority for your area. They will look into your complaint and give you a response. You also have the right to change your GP. If you wish to do so, fill in the appropriate section on the front of your medical card and give it to your new doctor; you do not have to have a special reason. If you have any difficulty registering with a new GP, contact the Family Health Service Authority who can appoint a GP for you if necessary.

The Mental Health Act Commission

Any patient detained in hospital under the Mental Health Act has the right to complain directly to the Mental Health Act Commission (in Scotland, the Mental Welfare Commission). Anyone, for instance a carer or relative, may also make a complaint to the Commission about the use of powers or the exercise of duties under the Mental Health Act. The Commission will look into the complaint and give a response.

The Mental Health Act Commission
Maid Marion House
56 Hounds Gate
Nottingham NG1 6BG
Tel: 0115 9504040

The Mental Welfare Commission (Scotland)
25 Drumsheugh Gardens
Edinburgh EH3 7RN
Tel: 0131 225 7034

Your MP

You may also contact your Member of Parliament, particularly if you have made complaints elsewhere which you feel have not been properly dealt with. Contact addresses are available from your local library.

Taking things further

If you have exhausted the avenues described above and want to take a complaint further, you may wish to consult a solicitor to discuss taking legal action. You can also ask for advice from the MIND legal department:

MIND Legal Department
Granta House
15–19 Broadway
London E15 4BQ
Tel: 0181 519 2122 (legal advice line Monday, Wednesday and Friday 2–4.30pm)

If your complaint is about health or social services, you may also write to the relevant Commissioner for the Health Service or for Local Administration (the Ombudsman); contact your local Citizens' Advice Bureau for the address.

12

Housing

Local authority housing • Housing associations • Other housing advice • Supported housing • Useful contacts

---

The NCVO (National Council for Voluntary Organisations) newsletter of April 1990 contained the following statistics: 'In the past ten years, 24,000 hospital beds have been closed but less than 4000 new residential places have been made available in the community'. Housing is an important part of community care, and yet there is a widespread shortage of affordable housing in Britain. People with mental health problems may experience particular difficulties in acquiring appropriate accommodation:

- mental health problems may affect your motivation, energy and practical ability to find suitable housing

- you may often have difficulty with getting employment, resulting in a low income and less choice in the housing market

- the stigma which surrounds mental illness may lead to discrimination, particularly with privately rented housing

- the range and availability of supported housing is very limited

For all these reasons, people often find themselves in unsuitable accommodation which can hinder rather than further their recovery from mental health problems. This chapter explains the various ways in which you can get access to the housing you need, whether independently in your own house or flat, or supported in a hostel or residential home.

LOCAL AUTHORITY HOUSING

Applying for housing

There are generally three ways in which you can apply for local authority housing:

WAITING LIST

Apply to go on your council's housing waiting list. To get priority you will need a letter from your doctor explaining your medical problems, how they are affected by current living circumstances, and how they will be helped by you being offered suitable accommodation.

PRIORITY FOR PEOPLE IN RESIDENTIAL CARE

Some councils operate schemes which give housing priority to people already in residential care, such as a hostel or group home whose social worker supports their application for more independent living. Talk to your local social services department to discover what schemes they operate.

HOMELESSNESS

Under the Housing Act 1985 all councils have a legal duty to provide accommodation for certain people who are homeless. Once you are accepted as homeless you will generally be offered temporary housing, which may be bed and breakfast, until a suitable permanent property becomes available. Some councils now also operate schemes which help you to find private rented housing. In order to be considered you must fall into both of these categories:

● unintentionally homeless or threatened with homelessness

● priority need

189

The first category means that, for instance, your parents or your landlord may have asked you to leave or you may be subject to violence where you are living. The local housing department will want some proof of the situation, such as a letter from your parents. They may also contact your last address to see whether they can arrange for you to go back there.

However, the housing department will not help you if you have done something deliberately so that you can apply for housing as a homeless person – for instance, deliberately failing to pay your rent so that the landlord evicts you, or leaving your previous accommodation just because you did not like it.

The second category, priority need, covers families with children, women expecting a baby, people over 60, and single people with medical or social problems (including problems with mental health) that make them vulnerable. However you will need proof, such as a letter from your doctor, when you go to the housing department.

DEALING WITH DIFFICULTIES
If you are genuinely homeless and have problems getting your local housing department to accept you, seek advice from your local CAB, law centre or advice centre. Not all local authorities apply the law in the same way, and their interpretation can sometimes be challenged successfully.

Getting a housing transfer

If you are already a council tenant and want to move, ask your local housing department about how to get a transfer. They are likely to want to know your reasons and whether your rent is up to date. You should also be able to register for a mutual exchange. For this you need to fill in a form, and you should be able to visit your housing department in order to look at a list of other people in your area who want an exchange. You can also talk to staff in the housing department if you want a transfer away from your local area, but it may be more difficult, depending on your reasons and their willingness to help.

HOUSING ASSOCIATIONS

There is a small but significant amount of housing association accommodation in Britain. This is similar to council accommodation but is owned by independent, non-profit-making organisations rather than the local authority. Local authorities also sometimes fund housing associations to build or renovate housing to which they can nominate people in need.

In areas of severe housing need, such as big cities, you will probably have to apply through your local authority's housing department, as described above, informing them that you are interested in a housing association tenancy as well as a council tenancy. In some parts of the country you may be able to apply direct to the housing associations' own waiting lists. Your local housing department should have a list of those in your area, as should the Housing Corporation (see p. 193).

OTHER HOUSING ADVICE

If you are a council tenant, the staff at your local housing department or district housing office should be able to advise you about maintenance, repairs, redecoration, fire safety, insurance and so on. In many areas tenants' handbooks are available.

Even if you are not a council tenant, many local authorities now have housing advice sections who can advise on all housing matters. This includes how to get private accommodation if you do not qualify for council housing; advice on problems with landlords, such as inadequate repairs or harassment; problems with noise and so on. Councils also have powers to intervene – for example, they can force landlords to maintain their properties and prosecute land-lords who try to get their tenants to move without following the proper legal procedures. Organisations such as Shelter can also give advice through their network of housing advice centres, or point people towards other independent sources of help (see the Useful Contacts section on p. 193).

SUPPORTED HOUSING

Some people find it difficult to manage in independent hous-ing and need more support. To cater for this need there is a variety of supported housing, ranging from staffed residen-tial care homes to shared houses which support staff visit occasionally. Supported housing may be run by the local social services, by voluntary organisations or by private home owners. There is wide variation in both availability and standard of accommodation and care. Some areas, for example some seaside towns, contain a large number of pri-vately run homes, often owned by ex-nurses. In other areas there may be no private homes at all.

Staffed residential care homes

This kind of 'home' or 'hostel' caters for people who need a lot of support from fellow residents and staff because they cannot manage on their own. Care of this type may be help-ful after a period in hospital as a way of building confidence before moving into more independent housing. Some people with longer-term needs may prefer to remain in residential care for many months or even years, although most residen-tial homes try to help people develop their abilities to the maximum and to achieve as much independence as possible.

Since April 1993 there has been a change in the way in which residential care is arranged. In the past people could be placed in residential homes, often some distance from their home area, without proper assessment of their needs. Under the new community care legislation an assessment of a person's needs by the local social services must now be made first. This means that residential care is more carefully planned, with individual needs being taken into account. More emphasis is also laid on arranging for local care rather than having people move to a strange area away from their family and friends.

TYPE AND STANDARD OF ACCOMMODATION

Standards in residential homes vary considerably. Some offer well-furnished single rooms, while others are of low standard despite the existence of inspection arrangements. Sizes range from small, usually privately run homes of three or four residents to larger homes with twenty to thirty residents.

In all these homes care and support should be available from staff according to your needs. This should be reviewed periodically at a meeting between yourself, the staff of the home and outside professionals such as a community psychiatric nurse or social worker.

HOW TO APPLY

If you need residential care you should ask your local social services to organise an assessment of your needs, usually by a social worker. This assessment should form the basis of arranging a suitable placement, whether in a local authority home or in one run by a voluntary organisation or a private individual. You should be fully involved in the process of choosing a home, and it is often helpful to visit a number to make comparisons. But the degree of choice will depend on where you live, and you may have to wait for a vacancy. The local authority is responsible for paying for your care, subject to an assessment of your means. Financial arrangements vary, although currently, if you are on benefit, you may be left as little as £13 a week for personal spending money.

Lodgings schemes

An alternative form of supported housing available in many

areas is a room in an ordinary house, where the householder offers a degree of support or care. This can be a successful arrangement for some people, although careful matching is important to make sure that people are compatible.

These schemes usually involve a payment by the local authority to the householder for the element of care and support provided, and regular support visits from a social worker or other professional.

HOW TO APPLY

As with residential care, this kind of supported housing is usually arranged after an assessment of needs by the local social services.

Unstaffed shared houses

Shared houses or flats are halfway between staffed residential care and fully independent housing. A great many schemes of this kind are run by social services, voluntary organisations such as MIND, and housing associations. The schemes aim to support people by providing tenancies in a house together with others who have experienced mental health problems. Tenants have their own bedroom and sometimes their own kitchen and bathroom; although there is often a shared lounge. The support from other tenants can be the most valuable aspect of this type of housing; usually some outside support is also given, in the form of regular visits from a housing worker or mental health professional. This is a popular and successful form of housing for many people, and may be either a stepping stone to full independence or a more permanent way of meeting housing need.

HOW TO APPLY

This type of housing is arranged through a tenancy for which rent is payable and housing benefit may be claimed. It does not usually involve any payment for 'care' and so a formal assessment of needs may not be required; you may be able to apply direct to the organisation concerned, who will have their own criteria for tenancies. To find out about schemes in your area, contact your local social services or branch of MIND.

Useful contacts

The main housing agencies for England, Wales, Northern Ireland and Scotland are listed below.

Housing Corporation (Head Office)
149 Tottenham Court Road
London W1P 0BN
Tel: 0171 2000

Can provide callers with a list of housing associations in their area, including those that run supported housing schemes.

Northern Ireland Housing Executive
2 Adelaide Street
Belfast BT2 8PB
Tel: 01232 240588

Offers advice and information on applying for public sector accommodation.

Scottish Homes (Head Office)
Thistle House
91 Haymarket Terrace
Edinburgh EH12 5HE
Tel: 0131 313 0044

Produces a regularly updated directory which lists all housing associations registered with Scottish Homes and a list of approved landlords in Scotland.

Tai Cymru (Housing in Wales)
25–30 Lambourne Crescent
Llanishen
Cardiff CF4 5ZJ
Tel: 01222 747979

Will supply a list of housing associations operating in various parts of Wales.

There are a number of other main independent sources or contacts for supported accommodation including:

Advance Housing and Support Ltd
2 Witan Way
Witney
Oxon OX8 6FE
Tel: 01993 772885

Provides accommodation and support within the community to meet the needs of people who have either a learning disability or a mental health problem. A directory of regional offices and staff is available.

Arbours Association
6 Church Lane
London N8 7BL
Tel: 0181 340 7646

A mental health charity which offers care, treatment and support to those in emotional distress. Its three long-term therapeutic communities are particularly suited to men and women with serious emotional and social problems but who are able to assume some social responsibility. Referrals come from all over the country, and other services include a short-stay crisis centre, training in psychotherapy and a clinic.

Association of Therapeutic Communities
14 Charterhouse Square
London EC1M 6AX
Tel: 0181 950 9557

Acts as a focus for information, debate, training and support for people who work in therapeutic communities or are interested in this way of working. A directory of therapeutic communities throughout the UK can be supplied. The contribution requested is currently £5.

Mental After Care Association (MACA)
25 Bedford Square
London WC1B 3HW
Tel: 0171 436 6194

MACA's services include two types of registered care home: those which the Association has set up and financed itself, and those set up in collaboration with other agencies to meet a specific local need. Referrals from any source are considered for their own projects, many of which provide, besides accommodation, a service to support people in their own homes. The primary aim of partnership projects is to meet local needs, but non-local placements may be available by negotiation with the agencies involved. A national list of schemes is available.

MACAbase is a database of residential care for people with mental health problems. To request a search of the database, telephone or write to the information officer at the above address. It is best to decide on the 'search criteria' (what information you need) beforehand. For example: Where should the home be? What sort of accommodation do you require? Do you need a structured programme of rehabilitation with intensive staff support? Is there an optimum period of stay? Detailed case histories are not necessary but some personal details would be helpful – e.g. age, sex, any facts which may affect the type of care approach required, and personal preferences about the accommodation sought. Details of suitable houses will then be sent out so that you can contact them direct to discuss suitability, fees and current vacancies. There is no charge for the MACAbase service, but donations are welcome.

MIND

Many local MIND groups or local associations for mental health have their own supported housing projects or are familiar with what is available in their area. For more information, ring national or regional numbers on p. 91–93.

Richmond Fellowship for Community Mental Health
8 Addison Road
London W14 8DL
Tel: 0171 603 6373

A registered charity and housing association with more than 56 projects throughout the UK for people with mental health and addiction problems. These projects include day care, employment, residential and supported housing communities. Details of services, lists of projects and information for prospective residents, including the criteria for selection, are available from the above address.

Some Richmond Fellowship houses cater for a wide age and diagnostic range, while others specialise in particular groups according to the amount of support needed. The latter includes houses for those with addiction problems, both alcohol and drugs; those diagnosed schizophrenic; young people; families with one or both parents and older people needing minimal support. Admission to a Richmond Fellowship house needs the recommendation of a social worker, probation officer or psychiatrist, and there must be a desire, or at least a willingness, to participate actively in the house programme. Programmes are aimed at helping residents to regain personal stability and the ability to make good relationships. The length of stay ranges from three months to five years, the average stay being about a year.

Shelter
88 Old Street
London EC1V 9HU
Tel: 0171 253 0202 (administration). Freephone 0800 446441
(London nightline emergency telephone advice service 365

days a year, staffed 6pm–9am during the week and round the clock at weekends and holidays)

The leading charity concerned with homelessness in Britain. Particularly concerned with vulnerable groups, Shelter has noted, for example, that during 1993 over 6710 families were accepted as homeless due to the mental illness of one of the family's members.

Shelter runs a training programme and can supply a list of books, reports, factsheets etc. on housing. It also has a network of 29 housing aid centres staffed by trained housing advisers who can offer help with every type of housing problem (details from the above address).

Shelter Cymru
25 Walter Road
Swansea SA1 5NN
Tel: 01792 469400

Shelter Scotland
8 Hampton Terrace
Edinburgh EH12 5JD
Tel: 0131 313 1550

Shelter in both Wales and Scotland campaigns for better services for homeless people, produces an extensive publications list and offers assistance through advice centres (details from the above addresses).

Stonham Housing Association Ltd
Octavia House
54 Ayres Street
London SE1 1EU
Tel: 0171 403 1144

Provides housing and support for a range of special needs, including people with mental health problems, in 250 small projects throughout England. Some are permanent homes, while others provide support which enables people to move to more independent accommodation. A comprehensive directory is available from the above address.

13

Money

**How problems can arise • Tackling money problems •
Coping with debts • Money advice • Extra help •
Welfare benefits • Mental incapacity •
Useful publications**

WHY MONEY IS IMPORTANT

Money is important to us all as a basic means of support,
and it gives us choices about what to buy or what to do.
Beyond this it can represent different things to different people: it may give opportunities for personal fulfilment; it may
represent a measure of personal value, worth or status; it
may give opportunities to compensate for other things going
wrong or to alleviate feelings of depression. But many people with mental health problems find themselves trapped on
low incomes, with careers interrupted through ill health, and
lack of money is often added to other stresses. This chapter
gives information about help in this area, and about the benefits system as it applies to people with mental health
problems.

HOW PROBLEMS CAN ARISE

Mental health problems and money problems often go
together. A lack of money can cause hardship and stress,
which may trigger mental health problems or make existing

200

ones worse. Anxiety and depression, as well as schizophrenia, can cause a loss of confidence and drive which makes it difficult for people to cope with their financial affairs. Gradually, with pressure from poor living standards and unpaid bills, this situation can get out of hand, producing a downward spiral which affects morale and impedes recovery. In extreme cases, if action is not taken, the person concerned may have their basic services such as gas and electricity disconnected, and be evicted.

Depending on the nature of the mental health problem, a person's earning power may be affected and he or she may need to claim state benefits. Unfortunately the benefits system is not as efficient as it should be, and does not always recognise special needs. For example, certain mental illnesses are 'episodic'; sometimes people may be very disabled, whereas at other times they are able to function relatively well. Their financial circumstances can fluctuate with their mental state, and they may often need to change their benefits claim. This means more form-filling and more opportunities for things to go wrong.

Particular problems can arise with some mental illnesses. For example, with manic-depressive illness it is quite common, during episodes when the person feels 'high', for them to buy things they cannot afford or give money away. This can lead to serious debt. Other mental illnesses can cause people to spend long periods at home, which increases their fuel bills. Some people have delusions or compulsions which raise their day-to-day expenditure, for example compulsive washing. But while such problems can seem overwhelming at the time, remember that there are a number of organisations which offer skilled advice, and that the most difficult money problems can usually be made more manageable.

TACKLING MONEY PROBLEMS

When money problems occur it is vital both to recognise the fact and to do something about it, seeking help or advice if needed. Money problems do not go away by themselves, and the head-in-the-sand approach does not work!

Getting information

Taking responsibility for your financial affairs is part of being in control of your life. It may therefore be a positive step to get the information you need and, as far as possible, to tackle the problems yourself. Books and leaflets from the sources listed below, and their telephone helplines, will give you detailed information.

• **The Department of Social Security (DSS) Benefits Agency** publishes free leaflets on the whole range of benefits available. These can be obtained direct from DSS offices, from larger post offices or from advice agencies, and are a good starting point. Leaflets are available in English and eleven other languages – Arabic, Bengali, Chinese, Greek, Gujarati, Hindi, Punjabi, Somali, Turkish, Urdu and Vietnamese.

• **Freephone DSS** is a confidential, free telephone service operated by the DSS. The service gives general information and advice about benefits, but cannot take up individual cases or get in touch with the local DSS offices. Phone 0800 666 555 (general advice); 0800 882 200 (disability benefits); 0800 289 011 (advice in Welsh); 0800 289 188 (advice in Urdu); 0800 521 360 (advice in Punjabi); or 0800 252 451 (advice in Chinese); in Northern Ireland, phone 0800 616 757.

• **The Child Poverty Action Group (CPAG)** publishes a range of comprehensive welfare benefits handbooks listed on p. 214.

• **Disability Alliance** is a voluntary organisation with expertise in welfare benefits which offers a telephone advice service for people with disability, including mental health problems. Tel: 0171 247 8776.

COPING WITH DEBTS

As with other money problems, it is best to tackle debts as early as possible, and you may wish to seek help from a Citizens' Advice Bureau or another advice agency. The steps to take are:

- write down your income from all sources; make sure all relevant benefits are claimed

- make a list of all essential expenses such as food, rent, gas and electricity, and see how much weekly income is left over; this can then be divided up to pay off debts in priority order

- contact all creditors and put them in the picture; ask them to hold off further action until they hear from you again

- decide which debts have highest priority (e.g. rent or mortgage payments, water charges and fuel,) and which have lower priority (e.g. hire purchase debts for non-essentials)

- contact your creditors in order of priority and try to agree a reasonable sum (weekly or monthly) which they will accept. Their main concern will be to get at least some of their money back, so they may be prepared to waive the interest payments.

- seek further advice if you cannot arrive at a reasonable agreement with any of your creditors

- if debts have arisen as a result of serious mental illness, it may be helpful for a professional such as a social worker to speak to your creditors and help in negotiations; in some cases it may even be possible to get your debts waived

- it is generally unwise to take out loans to stave off debts, as the interest charged is likely to add to the problem in the long term

Administration orders

If you have several debts you cannot deal with you may apply to the local county court for an administration order. This means your debts can be lumped together and you then pay a regular amount into court which is shared among the various creditors. Contact one of the organisations below for further advice.

MONEY ADVICE

Advice about money problems is available from the following agencies and from many other small local organisations. The Citizens' Advice Bureau, an independent agency offering a face-to-face service, may be the best place to start.

Citizens' Advice Bureau

CABs give free, impartial and confidential advice on welfare benefits, budgeting and debt counselling, as well as other issues. There are over a thousand local offices throughout the U.K. To find out where your nearest CAB is, look in the phone book, enquire at the local library or contact the appropriate head office:

National Association of CABs (England and Wales)
115 Pentonville Road
Myddleton House
London N1 9LZ
Tel: 0171 833 2181

Citizens' Advice Scotland
26 St George's Square
Edinburgh EH8 9LD
Tel: 0131 667 0156

Northern Ireland Association of CABs
11 Upper Crescent
Belfast BT7 1NT
Tel: 01232 231120

National Debt Line

A telephone advice service for people who are in debt. Tel: 0121 359 8501 (Monday and Thursday 10am–4pm, Tuesday and Wednesday 2–7pm)

Solicitors

A small but growing number of solicitors offer a welfare benefits advice service, funded through the Legal Aid system. Where this service is available it is often advertised in local newspapers.

Social services

Some local councils employ welfare rights advisers who offer a skilled advice service and can sometimes give considerable support to people in pursuing benefit claims. Where there are serious money problems, particularly when they relate to mental illness, advice can also be sought from a social worker. Indeed, they may be the best source of help, as they are likely to have a better understanding of the particular problems of people with mental illness, and to know the most effective ways of helping.

EXTRA HELP

Help from charities

If you have particularly pressing money problems and needs, you may be able to receive assistance from a charity. There are a number of charities, both national and local, which make small grants to individuals. Written application has to be made by a professional, usually a social worker. Information about grant-giving charities can be found in *A Guide to Grants for Individuals in Need*, edited by David Casson and Paul Brown, and published by the Directory of Social Change.

Clothing

The Women's Royal Voluntary Service (WRVS) runs a number of clothing stores where they distribute good-quality secondhand clothing free to people in need. You will normally need a letter of introduction from a social worker or other agency such as MIND. For your nearest branch look in the local phone book or contact the head office:

WRVS
234–244 Stockwell Road
London SW9 9SP
Tel: 0171 416 0146

Furniture

Some councils operate schemes for receiving unwanted furniture from local residents and redistributing this to people in need. There are also a number of local community furniture supply schemes through which reasonably priced secondhand furniture and household goods are available to people on low incomes. Again, you usually need to be referred by an agency such as social services or MIND.

Free bus passes

Under the Chronically Sick and Disabled Persons Act 1970, local authorities have a duty to provide assistance with travel permits for people who have a permanent and substantial disability, if the authority is satisfied that this is necessary. There is a wide variation in the way in which this duty is interpreted, and each council's social services department has its own criteria. In some areas travel permits are available to most people who are users of mental health services, while in others the policy is much more restrictive. For information about policy in your area, contact your local social services.

WELFARE BENEFITS

A range of welfare benefits is provided by the Benefits
Agency, which is part of the DSS (Department of Social
Security). The welfare benefits system is famous for being
complicated and it is hard to keep up with the regular
changes. However, if you are on benefits you should check to
see that you are receiving your full entitlement. With accurate information and good advice (see the section on money
advice above) it should be possible to make sure of this. This
section summarises the main benefits which are likely
to apply to people with mental health problems and their
carers.

Income support

This is a 'safety net' cash benefit to help people who do not
have enough to live on, and who are unemployed, unable to
work for health reasons or only able to work up to 16 hours
a week. People with savings over £8000 are not eligible for
income support.

- **premiums** are additions to the basic rate of income sup-
  port, which are payable in certain circumstances:
  - A **disability premium** can be added to income support if
    you or your partner receive invalidity benefit, severe dis-
    ablement allowance, mobility allowance or attendance
    allowance, if you are registered blind, or if you have sent
    in medical certificates for 28 weeks
  - A **carer premium** can be paid for carers receiving income
    support
  - **Other premiums** payable are for families with children,
    lone parents and pensioners

- **housing costs** are generally met through housing benefit
  (see p. 209). However, if you are on income support you
  can get help with mortgage interest payments and some
  other housing costs not covered by housing benefit

- **direct payments**: the Benefits Agency may be able to

arrange for direct payments for fuel and/or housing costs. This can be a helpful way of preventing arrears for some people

• **National Health Service charges** such as those for prescriptions, glasses or dental treatment are free if you receive income support

Family credit

This is a means-tested benefit payable to people who work more than 24 hours a week and have dependent children.

Social Fund

This fund is administered by the Benefits Agency to help people with expenditure which is difficult to pay out of regular income. Loans or grants can be made as follows:

• **crisis loans** are available in certain circumstances, for example if you have been burgled or lost all your money, and you have no other resources. You do not necessarily have to be on benefit to obtain a crisis loan. They have to be repaid. To apply for a crisis loan, contact the Social Fund section of your local Benefits Agency office.

• **budgeting loans** are available, if you are on income support, to help pay for an urgently needed item such as a cooker or a bed. They have to be repaid, for which purpose a small amount is deducted from your weekly income support. People with savings over £500, or over £1000 if they are aged 60 or more are not eligible.

• **community care grants** are available if you are on income support or expect to be on income support when moving into the community. They are designed to help people return to the community rather than to be in hospital or residential care homes; to help them stay in the community; or to ease exceptional pressures. The maximum awarded is usually in the region of £500, and the money does not have to be repaid. People with savings over £500, or over £1000 if they are aged 60 or more are not eligible.

Incapacity benefit

This benefit replaces the old sickness and invalidity benefits. People who have been unable to work through incapacity for up to 28 weeks receive the lower rate. The middle rate is payable from 29 to 52 weeks, and the higher rate for more than 52 weeks. It is awarded on the basis of an assessment of medical factors by Benefits Agency doctors, and only applies to people who have made sufficient national insurance contributions.

Housing benefit

This is for people who are living on benefits or a low income, and are paying rent. It is paid through the local council. Any income you have is taken into account in assessing the level of benefit, as are any savings over £3000; the upper savings limit is £16,000. If you are on income support you will usually get housing benefit for the full amount of your rent. For more details, contact the housing benefit section of your local council.

Council tax benefit

This benefit is available to help you meet your council tax bill if you are on a low income or disabled. Council tax is a tax on each household, not on individuals, but there are complicated rules whereby some people are not counted, for instance if they are 'severely mentally impaired'. People with a serious mental illness are sometimes accepted as coming into this category. If this applies to everyone in a household a 50 per cent discount is applied; a person living alone or with others who are not counted receives a 25 per cent discount. For more details, contact the council tax section of your local council who should have a detailed leaflet.

209

Disability living allowance (DLA)

DLA is a tax-free benefit for people under 65 who need help with personal care because of illness or disability. There are two parts to DLA: firstly for help with personal care, and secondly for help with mobility. The **care component** is assessed at higher, middle or lower rates according to your level of disability and your need for attendance or supervision by another person. The **mobility component** is paid at two rates to people who cannot walk, or cannot walk without supervision, are severely mentally impaired, or have severe behavioural problems.

DLA is an important benefit for people with a serious mental illness and is probably very much underclaimed. Decisions about awarding DLA to people with mental illness are often erratic, so when you fill out your application form take great care to describe your level of disability properly. Claims are assessed on the basis of advice from Benefit Agency doctors, who do not always seem to understand the issues and problems of mental illness. If your application for DLA is turned down, it may be worth asking for the decision to be reviewed.

Attendance allowance

This benefit now only applies to people whose illness or disability starts after the age of 65, and for which regular attention is needed from another person. A higher rate is payable where attention is needed 24 hours a day.

Severe disablement allowance (SDA)

SDA is payable to people between the ages of 16 and 60 who have been incapable of work for a minimum of 28 weeks, but are ineligible for incapacity benefit. You must be assessed as '80 per cent disabled' to qualify, unless your incapacity started before the age of 20. Rates of SDA are age-related, and are non-taxable.

Disability working allowance (DWA)

DWA is an income-related benefit for people who work at least 16 hours a week but have an illness or disability that limits their earning capacity. To claim, you must already be receiving another qualifying disability benefit.

Therapeutic earnings

If you are on income support or incapacity benefit and have an illness or disability you may be entitled to earn a limited amount without this being deducted from those two benefits. A doctor's letter is needed to confirm to the DSS that the work is of a therapeutic nature. In theory this should be helpful for people with a mental health problem who may find a small part-time job beneficial. In practice, however, it is of most use to the relatively small number of people who live rent-free, as therapeutic earnings are taken into account when assessing your eligibility for housing benefit.

Invalid care allowance (ICA)

ICA is a taxable benefit payable to people between 16 and pension age who are caring for a person who needs help and support for at least 35 hours a week. The person being cared for must already be receiving disability living allowance at the middle or higher rate for help with personal care, or attendance allowance. ICA is payable weekly, and there are additions for other adult or child dependents of the carer.

MENTAL INCAPACITY

When mental illness affects a person's ability to manage their own financial affairs it is usually only a temporary problem which is resolved when their health improves. Under these circumstances relatives, friends or professionals may be able to help until the person is able to manage on their own again. But where the problems are particularly serious or

211

persistent, more formal arrangements can be made.

Power of attorney

Anyone may authorise another person to act on their behalf by formally giving them power of attorney, which may be defined for a specific purpose or unlimited. The person granting power of attorney has to be mentally competent, and can cancel the arrangement at any time. If they later become mentally incapacitated, the power of attorney ceases to be valid. Contact a Citizen's Advice Bureau or solicitor for further information.

Enduring power of attorney

The Enduring Power of Attorney Act 1985 lays down the regulations for this power, under which the person appointed continues to exercise powers even when the subject becomes mentally incapacitated. When this happens there is a procedure which involves registering with the Court of Protection (see below) and giving notice to the person concerned and their relatives.

Appointeeship

Where a person is unable to manage their own affairs and is entitled to DSS benefits, another person can be made an appointee. Benefits are then paid to the appointee on behalf of the claimant. This arrangement is entirely at the discretion of the DSS, who will need to be satisfied that the person concerned is genuinely unable to manage their own benefits, and that the appointee is a suitable and trustworthy person.

The Mental Health Act, Section 142

Under this provision any income due to a person from any government source, including social security benefits, may be paid direct by the authority concerned to meet the debts or expenses of the person, or to the institution or person who is caring for them. This power can only be used on the basis of medical evidence that the person is 'incapable by reason of mental disorder of managing and administering his property and affairs'.

The Court of Protection

This court can make directions about the property and financial affairs of a person who is mentally incapacitated. Anyone can apply to the court on a person's behalf, although it is normally the person's nearest relative. On the basis of medical evidence the court may appoint a receiver, who may be a relative or the local authority, and who will be empowered to administer the person's financial affairs according to their best interests and the directions of the court. Where a person's assets are small, the Court of Protection may consider making a 'short procedure order', giving limited directions about a person's finances. Further information and application forms can be obtained direct from

Court of Protection
Public Trust Office
Stewart House
24 Kingsway
London WC2B 6JX
Tel: 0171 269 7000

USEFUL PUBLICATIONS

- *Balancing the Payments* by Alison Cobb, MIND, 1993. This MIND report describes the present social security system and makes recommendations for changes in the interests of people with mental health problems. It is available from: MIND Publications, Granta House, 15–19 Broadway, London E15 4BQ Tel: 0181 519 2122

213

- *The National Welfare Benefits Handbook*

- *The Rights Guide to Non-Means-Tested Benefits*
  These two detailed handbooks are published by the Child
  Poverty Action Group. New editions are published every
  April to take account of changes in the benefits system.
  Other CPAG publications include *The Fuel Rights
  Handbook, The Debt Advice Handbook, The Ethnic
  Minorities' Benefits Handbook* and *The Council Tax
  Handbook*. They are available from: Child Poverty Action
  Group, 4th Floor, 1–5 Bath Street, London EC1V 9PY Tel:
  0171 253 3406

- *The Disability Rights Handbook*
  This is another useful annual publication, published by
  and obtainable from: Disability Alliance, 1st Floor East,
  Universal House, 88–94 Wentworth Street, London
  E1 7SA Tel: 0171 247 8776

14

Employment and Training

Rehabilitation • Disability Employment Advisers • Help with finding employment • Sheltered employment • Training • Voluntary work

---

Having a job is not just about having extra money in your pocket, although this certainly makes life easier. A job also provides motivation and a reason to get out of bed in the morning. It offers purpose, social contact, status and a feeling of usefulness, and is good for self-esteem.

All this is as true for people with mental health problems as for anyone else. For some people, the prospect of full-time, permanent employment is an essential goal. For others, a more realistic target would involve steps towards gaining new skills and self-confidence in a sheltered training or employment setting. Although an appropriate job or training course can promote health and prevent further problems, inappropriate employment can be both as stressful and as damaging as unemployment. Unfortunately the choices are limited, and anyone looking for work can find it a depressing experience. There is some help and advice available, however, and the information below is intended to explain the options that exist.

215

Support in the workplace

Work can be stressful. Relationship problems, job security, dull and monotonous tasks, overwork or not being stretched enough can all add up and affect your mental well-being. It is in the interests of both you and your employer to consider how to reduce the causes of stress at work. Unfortunately, many employers share the same prejudices about users of mental health services as the wider population. There should be effective anti-discriminatory legislation for all people with disabilities, together with the opportunity to enter or re-enter paid work in a supported way. Just as the working environment for people with physical or sensory disability can be adapted to help with most problems, people who are emotionally vulnerable can and should be helped.

Good employers do what they can to promote the physical and mental health of their employees. This could mean arrangements for regular time off to keep appointments, access to confidential counselling, and suitable levels of supervision and support which recognise the stresses of the workplace.

Disclosing information to employers

One dilemma which you may be faced with if you had a 'psychiatric history' is whether to disclose this on an application form or during an interview. On the one hand, such disclosure could prejudice your chances of a job, or may affect the way colleagues relate to you. On the other hand, concealing information, particularly in response to a question about your mental health, could lead to your dismissal if it subsequently came to light. On balance, being truthful is usually the best course of action.

DISABILITY EMPLOYMENT ADVISORS

DEAs are based at many Jobcentres nationwide (see your local telephone directory). They offer advice to anyone between the ages of 16 and 65 who is experiencing difficulty in finding or keeping a job because of a disability or health problem, including a mental health problem. This service is also available to employed people who face problems at work which they wish to talk through with someone. It is always advisable to make an appointment before seeing a DEA.

DEAs usually offer an initial interview covering education, employment and relevant medical history and concentrating on the problems that might be anticipated in the workplace. This is called a Level One interview and lasts between one and one and one and a half hours. You can discuss the sort of work you want or, if you are unsure, career counselling may be available. The DEA can help with CVs and interview techniques, and discuss local opportunities for ordinary employment. They will also know about the availability of sheltered work or training and have details of employment rehabilitation centres, job introduction schemes and sheltered employment schemes (see below). Alternatively, you can simply talk to a DEA about your employment problems.

REHABILITATION

Employment rehabilitation centres

There are employment rehabilitation centres in most areas of the country which aim to offer a real-life work environment. If you want to assess whether you are ready for work, their programmes can help you to get back into the routine of work, including timekeeping and other disciplines. They can also help with updating skills. They do not, however, resolve the lack of employment opportunities for people with mental health problems.

217

HELP WITH FINDING EMPLOYMENT

Registering as disabled

If you have a long-term mental health problem you can apply to be included on the Disabled Persons' Register and receive a Green Card. A Green Card, which can only be obtained from a DEA, shows proof to employers that you are registered disabled and includes your registration number. Applications should be made through your DEA. There are two straightforward forms to fill in, one for the applicant (DP17), and one for a medical practitioner (DP32).

However, for many people with mental health problems registering as disabled is neither appropriate nor desirable, and the registration requirements have resulted in a low take-up of such schemes. Registration is voluntary and can be cancelled at any time.

As a registered disabled person you become eligible for particular work opportunities including job introduction schemes and sheltered employment schemes:

JOB INTRODUCTION SCHEMES

If an employer is unsure about taking on an employee with a disability, this scheme offers financial help towards the employee's wages for a trial period (usually six weeks).

SUPPORTED EMPLOYMENT SCHEMES

These schemes offer registered disabled people job opportunities or experience in open employment, in return for a full wage. If an employee is considered, for instance, '60 per cent efficient', the employer pays 60 per cent of the wages and a sponsor makes up the rest through the training agency.

Job clubs

These are open to people who have been unemployed for at least six months or who have been referred by a DEA. You should be ready to start a job when you go to the job club, and there is a referral procedure which will be explained at your Jobcentre or where you sign on. There is usually a wide range of job-hunting facilities on offer, including job leads, newspapers and other publications, telephone, postage and word processors. Training may also be available, involving mock interviews, preparation of CVs and application forms, and help with interview and telephone techniques.

Employment projects

Social services departments and organisations like MIND sometimes run local employment projects. Activities may include advising people on how to get into open employment, supporting people and employers in work placements, or providing people with relevant skills needed on the open market. Some projects are run like cooperatives, providing a range of activities from furniture restoration and light assembly to picture framing and cake decoration. A useful publication is *Working Out – the MIND Guide to Employment Projects*, which gives detailed information on almost 100 employment and training schemes in the UK and lists a further 250 projects; both sections are arranged alphabetically by county and metropolitan area, and it is still a useful guide even though it was published in 1988.

SHELTERED EMPLOYMENT

In the past, much 'sheltered work' merely served to occupy people's time in an unstimulating and unrewarding way. Today, however, many schemes such as those run by Remploy offer a variety of work experiences.

Remploy Ltd
Remploy House
415 Edgware Road
London NW2 6LR
Tel: 0181 452 8020

Remploy is the largest agency providing sheltered work

opportunities. It is a government-supported organisation which has over 90 factories throughout the UK, producing a variety of goods. Remploy aims to provide meaningful, sheltered employment for people with both physical and mental disabilities. Employees usually receive an average industrial wage and pay income tax, national insurance and so on. Most stay at Remploy on a long-term basis. There is a requirement to be registered disabled, and applications are made through the DEA at your Jobcentre. Remploy also has a section called Interwork, which finds open employment opportunities for people with disabilities.

TRAINING

Training and Enterprise Councils (England and Wales)

There are 82 Training and Enterprise Councils (TECs) which are private, locally based organisations. Through their contracts with the Department of Employment, TECs are responsible for managing local training and enterprise programmes, including Training for Work (See below), throughout England and Wales. TECs' functions also include assessing local labour market/business needs and developing new initiatives to meet them. They particularly aim to strengthen the skill base of the local community and to assist local enterprise to expand and compete effectively.

Local Enterprise Companies (Scotland)

LECs have a broader remit, than TECs. Through a contract with either of two organisations – Scottish Enterprise, or Highlands and Islands Enterprise – they are responsible for managing training and enterprise programmes, including Training for Work (see below), throughout Scotland. In addition, LECs also carry out the activities of the former Scottish Development Agency and the former Highlands and Islands

Development Board, which include development of property, urban renewal, help to businesses, land reclamation and environmental improvement.

TECs and LECs have to ensure that 'suitable high-quality training shall be available for all trainees who are shown by assessment to have disabilities or other significant personal disadvantages which give rise to special training needs'. They also have to ensure that training is given in a way which provides equal opportunities, and does not discriminate against people with mental health problems or any other group.

The Training for Work programme

This programme is aimed at unemployed adults aged 18 to 63. Individuals undergo a process of assessment and guidance to establish their suitability before joining the programme. Once on the programme, participants follow an agreed Individual Participation Plan. This may include a range of different types of training: aiming at National Vocational Qualifications or their equivalents, short work preparation courses, or training related to a particular job. The programme could also include a period of temporary work to help develop existing skills, or a mixture of training and temporary work. This individually tailored approach is especially helpful to people with special training needs who know from the outset that their particular needs are taken into account.

Most people with special training needs train alongside other participants. Sometimes special arrangements need to be made for people with disabilities, including mental health problems. These arrangements include:

● individual training packages where needed in particular cases

● adaptations to premises or equipment to meet the needs of a particular trainee

● special aids or equipment to help with training

221

- a personal reader service for visually impaired trainees

- a communication service for hearing-impaired trainees

- part-time training if an individual's capacity to train full-time is limited by their medical condition

- a grant of up to 75 per cent of the cost of fares to work is payable to certain severely disabled people whose disability prevents them from using public transport to get to work and requires them to use a taxi etc. There is an upper limit which can be checked with a DEA.

RESIDENTIAL TRAINING
This is available through 15 residential colleges for people with severe disabilities. It is offered to those who are considered to need a more supportive training environment because of the nature or severity of their disability.

PARTICIPATION ALLOWANCE
People participating in government training programmes are paid an allowance; this is currently the equivalent of their benefit plus a £10 premium, so that they are not worse off under Training for Work than they are when receiving benefit. They may also receive help with costs of travel to the place of training and other support costs.

Access to training

DEAs (see p.217) at Jobcentres will explain the full range of help available for those seeking employment or training. People with disabilities have priority for suitable places in Training for Work and can enter the programme without satisfying the 26-week unemployment requirement.

Services in Northern Ireland

Employment and training services in Northern Ireland are very similar to those in the rest of the UK. The main difference is that there are no LECs or TECs, (see p. 220) but the

Training and Employment Agency serves the same function and operates similar schemes. Sponsorship on a number of courses at residential training centres in mainland Britain is offered to people with special needs. The agency also provides financial support to a residential centre in Northern Ireland run by the Thomas Doran Parkanaur Trust, and to Enterprise Technology in Belfast. Details of other services, including local agency offices, can be obtained from:

Disablement Advisory Service
Training and Employment Agency
Clarendon House
9–21 Adelaide Street
Belfast
BT2 8DJ
Tel: 01232 541541

Voluntary work

This kind of work offers you the opportunity to gain skills and experience or to pursue your personal interests, as well as providing the satisfaction of being socially useful and helping others. It can be a way into a particular organisation or a new job, and you may be able to get a reference you can give to future employers.

There is a wide range of possibilities including nature conservation, youth work, driving, office work, shop work (particularly in charity shops), helping out in residential homes for the elderly, and assisting with children's play schemes. Voluntary work provides some of the same benefits as paid work, such as a structure to the day, social contact and so on. Arrangements for the payment of expenses are likely to be available. Contact the agencies below if you are interested.

National Association of Volunteer Bureaux
St Peter's College
College Road
Saltley
Birmingham B8 3TE
Tel: 0121 327 0265

This umbrella organisation has over 250 member local volunteer bureaux in England, Wales and Northern Ireland which can be contacted through the above address. All member bureaux are committed to the principle that everyone has a right to volunteer and they will do their best to find placements, no matter what the age of the applicant or their disability. Some bureaux have special needs workers whose brief includes supporting volunteers with mental health problems, but all bureaux are expected to take on this role. Most bureaux offer an initial, informal interview to discuss local opportunities and to see how these match up with the volunteer's interests and skills. The names and addresses of two referees are usually required.

Volunteer Development Scotland
80 Murray Place
Stirling FK8 2BX
Tel: 01786 479593

This is also an umbrella organisation, with over 150 member local bureaux or voluntary agencies in Scotland who can be contacted through the above address.

15

Education and Leisure

Adult education • Further education • Sports and physical activity • Looking after yourself • Other leisure activities • Holidays

---

There are now more opportunities than ever before for people to continue their education and to engage in leisure pursuits. This can be a positive way to stay mentally healthy and to keep the balance between activity and relaxation which most people need in their lives. Education and leisure should be seen not as therapies but as ordinary activities for everyone to pursue and enjoy. Lack of money may restrict your choices, but there may be help available if you are on a low income.

ADULT EDUCATION

The capacity to learn and to derive interest and fulfilment from learning continues throughout adult life, even though our formal education can cease as early as the age of 16 years. Many people who disliked school and could not wait to finish their formal education discover a thirst for knowledge later in life and find that adult education opens up new horizons.

225

Evening classes

In most areas of Britain there are local authority-run evening classes, and some daytime classes, in a wide range of subjects. For the vast majority you do not need any academic qualifications – just the time, the interest and the fee. Residents on low incomes or with a disability (including mental illness) are likely to be given discounts on the fees. These classes can be ideal for people who want to follow an interest or to develop a new one. They are usually friendly and informal and a good way of meeting other people. There is usually something for everyone, and the following list gives an idea of the subjects which may be available:

- **arts and crafts:** drawing, painting, pottery, flower arranging, dressmaking, needlework, picture-framing, woodwork, restoring furniture and upholstery

- **food and drink:** cookery, healthy eating, wine-making and wine-tasting

- **languages:** beginners' and more advanced classes in French, German, Spanish, Italian, Greek and sometimes other languages such as Punjabi, Urdu, Mandarin Chinese, Russian, Japanese and British Sign Language

- **business and information technology:** computing, word processing, typewriting, accountancy and book-keeping

- **hobbies and DIY:** photography, local history, tracing your ancestors, chess, bridge, video-making, calligraphy, car maintenance, creative writing and art appreciation

- **performing arts:** beginners' and more advanced tuition in playing the guitar and other instruments, jazz, dancing, music appreciation, drama, theatre studies and film studies

- **health and personal development:** meditation, religions, relaxation, massage, Shiatsu, Tai Chi, counselling, psychology, philosophy, assertiveness and self-defence

Basic literacy and numeracy

For one reason or another, some people leave school unable to read or write properly. Adult literacy classes are widely available and teach basic reading and writing skills; there are also more advanced classes for people who want to improve their grammar and spelling. Problems with numeracy are equally common, and there are often classes to help people develop skills in everyday maths. These basic courses can open up the world of education and study which is for everyone, not just the academically gifted.

How to find out more

Classes may be held at various local schools, colleges and other organisations. To find out about classes in your area and how to enrol, ask at your local library. The education department of your local authority will also have information. Most courses start in the autumn and the popular ones are quickly filled, so be prepared to move quickly.

Workers' Educational Association (WEA)

WEA (National Office)
Temple House
Victoria Park Square
London E2 9PB
Tel: 0181 983 1515

WEA (Scotland)
Riddle's Court
322 Lawnmarket
Edinburgh EH1 3PG
Tel : 0131 226 3456

WEA (Northern Ireland)
1 Fitzwilliam Street
Belfast BT9 6AW
Tel: 01232 329718

The WEA is a long-established organisation that provides adult education in a wide variety of subjects. There are over 800 branches throughout Britain. Despite the name of the organisation its classes are open to unemployed people as well as to those in work. Fees are greatly reduced for people on benefit.

Informal education

If you do not want to take a formal course or join a class, you can still follow an interest by studying on your own. Libraries are a rich source of information, and the staff are usually very helpful. For a small fee libraries will obtain books through the inter-library loan service if they do not have what you want on their own shelves.

FURTHER EDUCATION

For people who want to pursue more formal education, there are opportunities to do courses from a basic level right up to degree standard.

GCSEs (General Certificate of Secondary Education)

For GCSEs you will have to follow a course of study at either day or evening classes, and usually take a written examination. GCSEs can be taken either for their own sake, just for the achievement of a formal qualification, or to qualify for education at a higher level. As well as the more academic subjects there are courses in home economics, drama, media studies, craft, dress, textiles and many other areas.

GCE A-Levels (General Certificate of Education Advanced Level)

A-Levels involve more advanced study for people who have passed GCSEs. You normally take two or more subjects to qualify for entry to higher education. AS-Levels involve study at the same level but only cover about half the syllabus of an A-Level; two AS-Levels are equivalent to one A-Level.

NVQ and GNVQ (National and General National Vocation Qualifications)

NVQs are usually for people in employment who study part-time for a qualification in their particular field of work. GNVQs are related to a general area, not a specific job. There are different levels: GNVQ Foundation; GNVQ Intermediate; and GNVQ Advanced, for which four GCSEs or equivalent are needed. GNVQs can be taken in subjects such as building crafts, science, computing and information technology, catering, visual and performing arts, tourism, travel and leisure.

BTEC (Business and Technology Education Council)

BTEC and its Scottish equivalent awards diplomas and certificates in business and technological subjects at different levels. Diplomas are awarded for full-time courses, certificates for part-time. The BTEC First Certificate or Diploma is equivalent to four GCSEs; the National Certificate/Diploma is equivalent to two A-Levels; the Higher Certificate/ Diploma is at degree level.

City and Guilds

City and Guilds is a long-established organisation which sets examinations in craft and technical subjects, which involve both practical and academic work. There are three levels: Foundation Level, which takes two years' part-time study, Intermediate Level and National.

Educational Qualifications

First Level
GCSE
GNVQ Level 1
City and Guilds (Foundation)
BTEC First Certificate/Diploma (equivalent to four GCSEs)

Second Level
A-Levels
GNVQ Level 2

City and Guilds (Intermediate)
BTEC National Certificate/Diploma

Third Level
GNVQ Level 3
City and Guilds (National)
BTEC (Higher National Certificate/Diploma)
Degree (BA, BSc, etc.)

Other qualifications

There are other qualifications of various kinds which might be of interest. The Royal Society of Arts, for example, is an examination board which covers many vocational areas from basic skills to higher education. Many colleges and organisations offer their own certificates and qualifications.

Access courses

Many colleges now run what are called access courses, full-time or part-time. These are designed for people who do not have any formal qualifications, but want to go back to education to learn the basic skills of study and to acquire an introduction to the area they are interested in. There may also be 'back to work' courses for people who have been away from work for a time and want to brush up on work skills and basic English and maths.

How to find out more

Some of the courses described above may be open to adult learners in local sixth form colleges and schools. Otherwise, you are likely to find a variety of courses on offer at colleges of further and higher education, and at university extramural departments. Open University courses and other correspondence courses are another way of studying. The local library is a good starting point for information about colleges, which can then be contacted direct. Most are quite eager to promote their courses, and some have specialist staff who can advise people with a disability or special needs.

Sports and physical activity

Just as education is not just for the academically gifted, sports and physical activity are also for everyone. You do not have to be a natural athlete or to possess any special talent or competitive urge to be able to enjoy and benefit from your chosen activity.

The physical benefits of exercise

If you are physically fit you have more strength, suppleness and stamina to cope with the demands of day-to-day life and those occasions when a bit extra may be needed. Exercise increases the capacity and efficiency of your heart, blood vessels, lungs and muscles, which is good for long-term health and can help to protect you against heart disease and other illnesses. Exercise is also important if you are over-weight (some drugs prescribed for mental illness can cause weight gain).

Benefits to mental health

Regular exercise has been shown to increase self-confidence and self-awareness, and to reduce anxiety and depression. One of the most apparent benefits is the 'feel good' factor that comes from physical activity. After fairly vigorous exercise it is normal to have a feeling of well-being; this can lead to an enjoyable sense of ease and social confidence which may surprise people who know you. It has been suggested that this is in part caused by the body producing increased levels of a substance called Beta-Endorphine.

The range of activities available

There is an enormous variety of activities to choose from, some of which involve joining with other people while others can be enjoyed by yourself. Here is a list of suggested activities which may be available:

- **activities involving other people:** badminton, tennis, basketball, bowls, golf, table tennis, dance exercise, aerobics, keep-fit classes, watersports, yoga and Tai Chi classes

- **activities you can enjoy by yourself:** swimming, weight training, keep-fit and aerobics (video), jogging, cycling, walking, exercise bike

How to get started

If you are not physically fit to start with, it is important to build up your exercise programme only gradually. If you have any concerns about your health, for example if you have an illness or you are taking medication, ask your doctor for advice. A reasonable level of physical fitness can generally be maintained by taking fairly vigorous exercise two or three times a week.

Information about sports and leisure facilities in your area can be obtained from your local library or sports and leisure centre. Qualified instructors are likely to hold classes in many activities. It may be possible for users of mental health services to join together and make block bookings at a discount. Otherwise leisure passes are usually available to people on low incomes, allowing them to use facilities at a discount. There are a small number of schemes in the UK where GPs can refer people to the local leisure centre if they are unfit or overweight, and 'prescribe' vouchers for swimming and other activities.

Portsmouth Interaction
Recreation Division
Guildhall
Portsmouth PO1 2AD
Tel: 01705 873142

232

An example of a service which helps people with mental health problems to get involved in sports and leisure activities. The members decide what activities they want to take part in and leisure staff (not mental health professionals) are on hand to help and give instruction. Activities include swimming, badminton, ten pin bowling, horse riding, country walks and camping, and take place in normal leisure facilities so that members are seen as ordinary people doing ordinary things.

LOOKING AFTER YOURSELF

Diet

Physical fitness is just one aspect of looking after yourself. It is equally important to have a healthy, balanced diet. The Health Education Authority has produced eight guidelines for healthy eating:

- enjoy your food
- eat a variety of foods
- eat the right amount to be a healthy weight
- eat plenty of foods rich in starch and fibre
- don't eat too much fat
- don't eat sugary foods too often
- keep an eye on the vitamins and minerals in your food
- if you drink alcohol, keep within sensible limits

Smoking

This is a major cause of serious illness, and a very expensive habit for people on low incomes. Giving up smoking is not easy, but it may be the single most important thing you can do to improve your health. Your GP or health centre should be able to offer advice on breaking the habit. There are also telephone helplines for smokers seeking advice, counselling and referral to local stop-smoking groups (see pp. 161–2).

OTHER LEISURE ACTIVITIES

Pursuing an interest to the point where you become knowledgeable or skilful can be very satisfying, and some activities are simply enjoyable in themselves. Apart from the range of adult education and physical activities mentioned above there is an endless list of other pursuits, from indoor activities such as board games, snooker and darts to outdoor pursuits such as bird-watching and conservation. One of the most popular of all hobbies is gardening, and for those without gardens allotments can be rented in many areas for a low cost; contact your local council for information.

Travel permits

Many people with mental health problems are able to benefit from travel permits issued by the local social services. These allow free use of local public transport. People who are 'permanently and substantially disabled' may qualify for this, although in practice there is wide variation between authorities some of whom are relatively generous in issuing permits to people with mental health problems, and some of whom are not. Travel permits can open up leisure possibilities which might otherwise be too costly.

Entertainment

The cost of entertainment can be quite high, but some areas have special discount or leisure pass schemes for people with mental health problems. Some of these include reductions or refunds on cinema, theatre and concert tickets. Your local library will have information about free or inexpensive events; many libraries publish a regular 'What's On' leaflet. Most libraries also have a lending service for videos and cassettes.

Holidays

Everyone needs a break from time to time, and holidays are something to look forward to. The main problems for people with mental health problems are likely to be a need for special support and for help with the cost.

Holiday Care Service
2 Old Bank Chambers
Station Road
Horley
Surrey RH6 9HW
Tel: 01293 774535

Provides an information service on holidays and travel for people with a disability.

Arranging your own holiday

Inexpensive holidays can be arranged in hotels, guest houses, self-catering apartments and caravans in popular resorts, particularly if you book outside the peak season. Telephone the tourist information office for the area you are interested in and ask them to send a list of accommodation within your price bracket.

Help with the cost

Some local authorities run their own subsidised holiday schemes. They also have the power to give financial assistance towards the cost of a holiday for people with disabilities. Unfortunately the funds tend to be very limited and not many people with mental health problems get direct help in this way. If you are in touch with a social worker it may be possible for him or her to obtain a grant for you from a charity.

Retreats

Some people go to retreats for religious reasons, but this is not usually a requirement. They offer an opportunity to get away from the stress and strain of everyday life and spend time quietly reflecting or relaxing. A list of retreats can be obtained from:

The National Retreat Association
Liddon House
24 South Audley Street
London W1Y 5DL
Tel: 0171 493 3534

Respite care

For people who need special support or care, respite care can be arranged in a residential home. Local authority social services may be able to arrange this, and to help with the cost.

Appendix 1:
Terms Used in
Psychiatry

A lot of technical terms (or jargon) are used in psychiatry, sometimes to describe quite simple things. This inability to use plain English does not help psychiatrists in their task of communicating clearly with people. This list will help to demystify some of the language of psychiatry. It does not include certain terms which are explained elsewhere in this book, and which can be looked up in the index.

Abreaction   a release of repressed feelings

Acute   a serious condition which arises suddenly

Affect   mood

Akathisia   restlessness; a common side-effect of some antipsychotic drugs

Amnesia   loss of memory; can be caused by head injury, or can occur briefly for no apparent reason in mid to late life

Anankastic   obsessive-compulsive personality

Aphasia   loss of the power of speech

Autism   a form of *learning disability* in which the person appears to live in a world apart, and has difficulty in communicating and developing normal relationships

Avoidance   a coping strategy in which the person avoids thinking or talking about something which is causing anxiety

Briquet's syndrome a severe form of *conversion disorder or dissociative disorder* in which the person experiences many physical symptoms for long periods, but without apparent physical cause

Cataplexy a brief period of paralysis which may occur without physical cause

Catatonia a state in which the person barely moves, or adopts strange postures

Chemotherapy drug treatment

Chronic a condition which is of long duration

Cognitive related to thinking, e.g. cognitive therapy

Confabulation where a person who is confused or forgetful makes things up to fill in the gaps in a conversation

Conversion disorder a state in which physical symptoms are experienced which have a psychological cause, e.g. loss of vision, or loss of feeling or power in a limb. Also known as *hysteria* or *dissociative disorder*

Coprolalia uttering obscenities

Cranial relating to the brain (the cranium)

Cyclothymia mood swings

Cyclothymic personality a personality type where mood swings predominate

Delusion a false belief which is firmly held

Dementia an irreversible deterioration of brain function, affecting memory, thinking and reasoning

Dependence (of drugs) being physically dependent on a drug so that symptoms occur if the drug is stopped or reduced

Depersonalisation a feeling of being unreal and detached

Depot medication medication given by injection into the muscle tissue, from where it is slowly released

Derealisation a feeling that other people and objects have lost their normal qualities

Desensitisation a technique of behaviour therapy involving gradual exposure to the thing or situation which is causing anxiety

Displacement a defence mechanism where feelings are transferred unconsciously, e.g. picking a quarrel with your partner after a bad day at work

Dissociative disorder sometimes used with the same meaning as *conversion disorder* and *hysteria*

Dysmorphophobia a condition in which a person has an exaggerated or false perception that a part of their body is abnormal, e.g. the shape of the nose

Dysphasia difficulty in talking

Echolalia repetition of words or phrases which have been heard

Elective mutism refusing to speak

Endogenous originating within the person, not from external cause, e.g. endogenous depression

Exogenous caused by a reaction to external influences, e.g. exogenous depression

Factitious disorder deliberate feigning of symptoms, physical or psychiatric, so as to be diagnosed ill

Flooding a technique of behaviour therapy which involves a rapid exposure to the thing or situation which is causing anxiety

Forensic psychiatry a specialist branch of psychiatry concerned with people who have committed criminal offences

Fugue state a temporary state of disorientation and memory loss; it can occur with epilepsy, severe depression and alcoholism

Hallucination an abnormal perception with no basis on reality; most commonly auditory (hearing voices), but can be visual, or involve taste, smell or touch

Hebephrenic syndrome a category of schizophrenia now seldom used, describing symptoms of mood and thought disorder and hallucinations

Histrionic a personality type: lively, sociable, dramatic, sometimes attention-seeking and selfish

Hyperventilation very rapid, shallow breathing, which causes dizziness and other physical symptoms, and can increase anxiety

Hypochondria   having excessive anxiety about one's health

Hypomanic   literally means 'less than manic', and is often used to describe symptoms of mania

Hysteria   a state where mental or physical symptoms are caused by psychological factors of which the person is unaware. Also known as *conversion disorder* or *dissociative disorder*

Illusion   a misperception of the senses based on an actual occurrence which is wrongly interpreted

Insomnia   inability to sleep

Knight's move thinking   a psychotic symptom where logical connections between ideas appear to be lacking and the person's thinking is indirect (as in the chess move) and muddled

Labile   unstable (usually referring to mood swings)

Learning disability   this is not a mental illness and refers to a permanent condition in which the development of the brain is affected; it used to be known as mental handicap

Multiple personality   a very rare condition in which a person takes on additional distinct personalities, e.g. Jekyll and Hyde

Munchausen's syndrome   a condition in which the person continually seeks treatment for illnesses which they do not have, and may go to considerable lengths, including self-injury, to get admitted to hospital

Munchausen's syndrome by proxy   a condition in which a person seeks treatment for another (e.g. a parent for a child) for an illness they do not have; this may involve inflicting harm on the person

Mutism   not speaking

Narcissistic   a personality type: self-admiring and self-important, preoccupied with own powers and abilities, seeking attention from others

Narcolepsy   extreme drowsiness; falling asleep repeatedly

Neologism   a new word, or a word used with special meaning, e.g. by a person who is psychotic

Neurosis   a mental disorder related to an emotional state, anxiety, depression, distress or obsession where the person has some insight into their problems

Nihilistic delusion   a delusion that a person or thing does not exist; or a general or specific feeling of doom

Organic (of mental disorder)   caused by physical illness, injury or damage

Othello syndrome   irrational and extreme jealousy as a result of a false belief that one's partner is being unfaithful

Paranoia   a state in which the person suffers from delusions which may include unwarranted suspicion and feelings of being persecuted

Paraphrenia   a term of uncertain validity, used by some psychiatrists to describe schizophrenia which starts late in life and in which there are delusions without any accompanying changes in personality

Parasomnia   a sleep disturbance, e.g. nightmares or sleep-walking

Passive-aggressive   describes behaviour or personality which is very obstructive and uncooperative but without aggression, e.g. avoiding, delaying tactics, allied to unreasonably critical attitude towards others

Pathological   related to illness or disorder

Perseveration   where a person repeats the same words or actions, or has a recurring idea

Post-traumatic stress disorder   describes the problems experienced by people who have been involved in a traumatic event, e.g. experiencing flashbacks or nightmares, avoidance behaviour and other emotional effects

Prognosis   the likely outcome of an illness

Psychodrama   a kind of drama therapy which involves role-playing situations which are of particular significance to the person

Psychogenic   of psychological rather than physical cause

Psychosis   a mental disorder which involves a serious distortion of the person's thought processes and capacity to recognise reality

Psychosomatic where a physical symptom is caused by emotional or psychological factors

Regression reverting to behaviour more appropriate to an earlier stage of development, e.g. childish

Schizoid personality a personality type: emotionally cold, unsociable and detached

Seasonal affective disorder a disorder in which depression is caused by a lack of exposure to sunlight; it can be treated by using artificial light

Simple schizophrenia a category describing symptoms of loss of social skills and motivation; now seldom used and of doubtful validity

Somatic refers to physical sensation as opposed to sensation in the mind

Somatisation where physical symptoms are caused by emotional or psychological problems

Stereotypies repeated odd movements, sometimes made by people with chronic schizophrenia

Stupor a state in which the person does not speak, move or respond

Syndrome a group of symptoms which indicate a particular illness or condition

Tachyphasia rapid speech

Tolerance (of drugs) where, with continued used, a drug loses it effectiveness, e.g. anti-anxiety drugs

Tourette syndrome a distressing condition in which the person has symptoms which may include facial tics and other strange movements, and an uncontrollable compulsion to make noises or utter swearwords; treatment is likely to involve behavioural/cognitive therapy

Transference where a patient in psychoanalysis transfers feelings about significant people (e.g. parents or partners) on to the therapist

Appendix 2: Directory of Organisations

The following is a list of useful mental health organisations which do not appear elsewhere in the book. A complete alphabetical index of all organisations listed is on pp. 246–50.

Action on Phobias Association (Scotland)
6 Grange Street
Kilmarnock KA1 2AR
Tel: 01357 22274
Information and support; local groups

AMNASS (Amnesia Association)
7 King Edward Court
King Edward Street
Nottingham
NG1 1EW
Tel: 0115 9240800

Anorexia and Bulimia Nervosa Association
Women's Health Centre
Tottenham Town Hall
Approach Road
London N15 4RB
Tel: 0181 885 3936 (helpline Wednesday 6–8pm)

Cyclothymics
36 Lorn Road
London SW9 0AD
Tel: 0171 733 7912

Support to people who suffer mood swings

Department of Health
Richmond House
79 Whitehall
London SW1A 2NS
Tel: 0171 210 3000

Ex-Services Mental Welfare Society (COMBAT STRESS)
Broadway House
The Broadway
London SW19 1RL
Tel: 0181 543 6333
Supported housing and respite care

Gerda Boyesen Centre for Biodynamic Psychology
Acacia House
Central Avenue
The Vale
London W3 7JX
Tel: 0181 746 0499

HEADWAY, The National Head Injuries Association
7 King Edward Court
King Edward Street
Nottingham NG1 1EW
Tel: 0115 9240432
Education, support, local groups

Huntington's Disease Association
108 Battersea High Street
London SW11 3HP
Tel: 0171 223 7000
National charity concerned with Huntington's Chorea

Institute of Psychiatry
De Crespigny Park
London SE5 8AF
Tel: 0171 703 5411
The leading centre of research and practice in psychiatry

King's Fund Centre
126 Albert Street
London NW1 7NF
Tel: 0171 267 6111
Policy development in health and social services

Lincoln Centre and Institute for Psychotherapy
19 Abbeville Mews
88 Clapham Park
London SW4 7BX
Tel: 0171 978 1545
Clinical service, training

Matthew Trust
PO Box 604
London SW6 3AG
Tel: 0171 736 5976
Campaigning organisation for mentally disordered offenders

Mental Aftercare in Registered Care (MARCH)
Town Hall
Newark
Notts NG24 1DU
Tel: 0636 611261 (gen enq)
Tel: 0636 611270 (national bed vacancy register)
Represents independent proprietors; supplies placement information

Mental Health Foundation
37 Mortimer Street
London W1N 7RJ
Tel: 0171 580 0145
Fundraising; promotes research and projects

Mental Health Media Council
356 Holloway Road
London N7 6PA
Tel: 0171 700 0100
Information and advice; range of videos on mental health

Northern Ireland Agoraphobia and Anxiety Society
143 University Street
Belfast
BT7 1HP
Tel: 01232 235170

Patients' Association
18 Victoria Park Square
London E2 9PF
Tel: 0181 981 5676
Charity representing patients;
gives advice on rights and
complaints

Phobics' Society
4 Cheltenham Road
Chorlton-cum-hardy
Manchester M21 1QN
Tel: 0161 881 1937
Information and advice; local
groups

**Psychiatric Rehabilitation
Association**
Boyford Mews
Boyford Street
London E8 3SF
Tel: 0181 985 3570
Provides services, research and
training

Royal College of Psychiatrists
17 Belgrave Square
London SW1X 8PG
Tel: 0171 235 2351

**Sainsbury Centre for Mental
Health**
134–138 Borough High Street
London SE1 1LB
Tel: 0171 403 8790
Mental health promotion;
information, research and
training

**Schizophrenia Association of
Great Britain**
International Schizophrenia
Centre
Bryn Hyfryd
The Crescent
Bangor
Gwynedd LL57 2AG
Tel: 01248 354048
Information, research

**Tourette Syndrome (UK)
Association**
169 Wickham Street
Welling
Kent
DA16 3BS
Tel: 0181 304 5446
Information and support;
promotes awareness about TS

**Women in Special Hospitals and
Secure Units**
25 Horsell Road
London N5 1XL
Tel: 0171 700 6684
Information and advice;
campaigning

Women's Therapy Centre
6–9 Manor Gardens
London N7 6LA
Tel: 0171 263 6200
Information and education
(national); psychotherapy
(London)

Index of Organisations

All the organisations and agencies referred to in the text or in the directory of organisations on p. 243 are listed here.

Index